English for the Global Workplace

CEFR A2

Kayoko Shiomi
Matthew Coomber
LiveABC editors

photographs

iStockphoto

StreamLine

Web 動画・音声ファイルのストリーミング再生について

CD マーク及び Web 動画マークがある箇所は、PC、スマートフォン、タブレット端末において、無料でストリーミング再生することができます。下記 URL よりご利用ください。再生手順や動作環境などは本書巻末の「Web 動画のご案内」をご覧ください。

https://st.seibido.co.jp

音声ファイルのダウンロードについて

CD マークがある箇所は、ダウンロードすることも可能です。下記 URL の書籍詳細ページにあるダウンロードアイコンをクリックしてください。

https://www.seibido.co.jp/ad717

English for the Global Workplace

Copyright © 2024 LiveABC Interactive Corporation
Japanese edition copyright © Seibido Publishing Co., Ltd, Japanese edition
All rights reserved.

All rights reserved for Japan.
No part of this book may be reproduced in any form
without permission from Seibido Co., Ltd.

CONTENTS

	Content Chart	4
	Overview	6
	Introduction	8
UNIT 1	Meeting for the First Time	9
UNIT 2	Welcoming a Newcomer	17
UNIT 3	Telephone Communication	25
UNIT 4	Office Issues	33
UNIT 5	Arranging a Meeting	41
UNIT 6	Video Conferencing	49
UNIT 7	Review 1	57
UNIT 8	Job Interviews	63
UNIT 9	Traveling on Business	71
UNIT 10	Receiving Overseas Visitors	79
UNIT 11	Meeting with Clients	87
UNIT 12	Negotiations	95
UNIT 13	Giving Presentations	103
UNIT 14	Review 2	111
	LINGUAPORTA	118
	StreamLine	119

CONTENT CHART

UNIT	TOPIC	LEARNING GOALS	DIALOGUES / TALKS	PAGES
1	Meeting for the First Time	• Greeting visitors • Making visitors feel welcome	*Scene 1:* At Reception *Scene 2:* Meeting Company Guests	9-16
2	Welcoming a Newcomer	• Introducing your work environment • Informing someone of company rules	*Scene 1:* Work Environment and Facilities *Scene 2:* The Company's Rules	17-24
3	Telephone Communication	• Answering the phone and connecting a caller • Rescheduling a meeting time	*Scene 1:* Incoming Calls *Scene 2:* Rescheduling an Appointment	25-32
4	Office Issues	• Asking for leave • Working overtime and covering shifts	*Scene 1:* Taking Time Off *Scene 2:* Finding a Replacement	33-40
5	Arranging a Meeting	• Planning a meeting • Reserving a meeting space and supplies	*Scene 1:* Meeting Preparations *Scene 2:* Making Arrangements	41-48
6	Video Conferencing	• Making video calls • Dealing with problems	*Scene 1:* Online Meeting *Scene 2:* Problem Solving	49-56
7	Review 1			57-62

UNIT	TOPIC	LEARNING GOALS	DIALOGUES / TALKS	PAGES
8	Job Interviews	• Answering questions and promoting yourself in a job interview • Asking about the job and the company	Scene 1: Talking about Yourself Scene 2: Asking about the Job	63-70
9	Traveling on Business	• Arriving at the airport • Checking into a hotel	Scene 1: Being Picked Up Scene 2: Accommodations	71-78
10	Receiving Overseas Visitors	• Picking up a visitor • Showing a visitor around your workplace	Scene 1: At the Airport Scene 2: A Company Tour	79-86
11	Meeting with Clients	• Introducing a company's history • Giving information about products and services	Scene 1: Company Introductions Scene 2: Introducing Products and Services	87-94
12	Negotiations	• Asking for a better or lower price • Confirming payment terms	Scene 1: Bargaining Scene 2: Completing the Order	95-102
13	Giving Presentations	• Giving a presentation to introduce your company • Explaining tables, charts, and graphs	Scene 1: Giving a Successful Presentation Scene 2: Pie Charts	103-110
14	Review 2			111-116

OVERVIEW

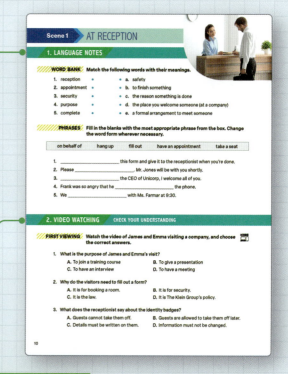

CHECKLIST

Lists the key learning points of the unit.

WARM-UP

Introduces the topic through exercises that encourage learners to share existing ideas. A video overview of each unit is available.

LANGUAGE NOTES

Contains key words and phrases from the dialogues. Students are asked to match key words in the Word Bank with their definitions and choose the most appropriate phrases to fill the gaps in example sentences.

VIDEO WATCHING

Shows two videos of business scenes. Students watch the video and answer follow-up questions to check their comprehension.

DIALOGUES / TALKS

Includes authentic materials which model real-life business scenarios while providing key language associated with the topic. Students watch the video, fill in the blanks, and practice the conversations.

USEFUL EXPRESSIONS

Demonstrates how to use essential expressions from the dialogue in a variety of contexts. Students match the responses with the questions or statements, put them in a natural order, or practice shadowing given expressions.

LANGUAGE PRACTICE

Gives students the opportunity to apply what they have learned and express themselves through controlled practice in a realistic speaking scenario.

LANGUAGE FUNCTION

Focuses on grammatical and functional use of certain words or phrases in given situations.

READING COMPREHENSION

Provides a reading passage related to the topic of each unit. Students read a passage and answer true-false or multiple-choice questions to check their comprehension.

ACTIVE LEARNING

Offers students the opportunity to utilize what they have learned. They are encouraged to use integrated English skills, plan and perform role plays, make presentations, and participate in student-centered creative activities.

INTRODUCTION

Welcome to *English for the Global Workplace*. In our increasingly globalized society, competency in English is essential not only in the academic world, but also in the business sector. Whatever your English learning goals, this book will help you to reach them.

As the title suggests, *English for the Global Workplace* is focused on business-related subjects. It covers a wide range of topics, from situations such as greeting visitors and welcoming new coworkers, to essential language for business meetings, video conferencing, making presentations, etc. The book also includes realistic business dialogues presented in video format.

English for the Global Workplace is divided into fourteen units, including two review units with TOEIC exam style exercises. Each unit has clearly-stated objectives and follows a defined structure. Units are divided into the following parts:

- Warm-Up: Introductory activities
- Language Notes: Word bank and phrases
- Video Watching: Conversations in different business scenarios
- Useful Expressions: Matching questions and responses, shadowing, sequencing of conversations, and completion of sentences
- Language Practice: Creating your own dialogue based on a sample and practicing the conversations in a pair
- Language Function: Focusing on the grammar and usage of certain words and expressions
- Reading Comprehension: Reading passages with T/F and multiple-choice questions
- Active Learning: Student-centered activities integrating the skills learned in each unit, including role-plays, presentations, and creative writing tasks.

In today's world, no matter where you live or what you do for a living, you will almost certainly encounter English. *English for the Global Workplace* gives you the opportunity to practice four important language skills: listening, speaking, reading, and writing, and provides you with the tools you need to feel comfortable communicating in English in any business situation.

UNIT 1
Meeting for the First Time

✓ Checklist

In this unit, you will learn about...
- Greeting visitors
- Making visitors feel welcome

Warm-up

1. Fill in the blanks with the most appropriate word from the box to complete the reasons a company may require a visitor to wear a visitor's pass. (There is one extra word in the box.)

Improved Security	Future Planning and Reference
• to _____ track of all the visitors • to _____ if someone who shouldn't be there is walking around	• to _____ on something with a visitor • to _____ a future meeting with a visitor for another reason

schedule   identify   keep   contact   follow up

2. Work in a pair. Look at the visitor pass below and ask questions about the visitor's name, his/her company, the purpose of the visit, and the appointment time.

VISITOR PASS

NAME	Casey Jones
COMPANY	Attica Marketing
REASON FOR VISIT	TV commercial meeting with Shawn Turner in Marketing
APPOINTMENT	10:00 a.m.
TIME IN	9:50 a.m.	TIME OUT	11:10 a.m.
DATE	5/8

Scene 1 — AT RECEPTION

1. LANGUAGE NOTES

WORD BANK Match the following words with their meanings.

1. reception
2. appointment
3. security
4. purpose
5. complete

a. safety
b. to finish something
c. the reason something is done
d. the place you welcome someone (at a company)
e. a formal arrangement to meet someone

PHRASES Fill in the blanks with the most appropriate phrase from the box. Change the word form wherever necessary.

on behalf of	hang up	fill out	have an appointment	take a seat

1. _____ this form and give it to the receptionist when you're done.
2. Please _____. Mr. Jones will be with you shortly.
3. _____ the CEO of Unicorp, I welcome all of you.
4. Frank was so angry that he _____ the phone.
5. We _____ with Ms. Farmar at 9:30.

2. VIDEO WATCHING — CHECK YOUR UNDERSTANDING

FIRST VIEWING Watch the video of James and Emma visiting a company, and choose the correct answers.

1. What is the purpose of James and Emma's visit?
   A. To join a training course
   B. To give a presentation
   C. To have an interview
   D. To have a meeting

2. Why do the visitors need to fill out a form?
   A. It is for booking a room.
   B. It is for security.
   C. It is the law.
   D. It is The Klein Group's policy.

3. What does the receptionist say about the identity badges?
   A. Guests cannot take them off.
   B. Guests are allowed to take them off later.
   C. Details must be written on them.
   D. Information must not be changed.

UNIT 1 *Meeting for the First Time*

SECOND VIEWING   Watch the video again and fill in the blanks with the words below.

  1-02

| for a meeting | have your names | have an appointment |
| must be worn | this visitor form | |

James and Emma walk through an entrance into the reception area of a large company.

Receptionist: Hi there. How may I help you?

James: We're here on behalf of The Klein Group. We ① _____ with Ms. Farmar at 10:30.

Receptionist: OK. Could I ② _____, please?

James: I'm James Davis and this is Emma Smith.

Receptionist: Great. I just need you to fill out ③ _____ for security purposes. Please write your full names, company, telephone number, and purpose of the meeting.

James: Sure. No problem.

(The receptionist calls Ms. Farmar while the guests complete the form.)

Receptionist: Hi, Josephine. I'm with James Davis and Emma Smith from The Klein Group. They're here ④ _____ with you at 10:30. *(Pause)* Yes, OK. Will do. Thanks. *(Hangs up the phone)* I've got a couple of identity badges for you which ⑤ _____ at all times. Here you are. Please take a seat over there, and Ms. Farmar will be with you shortly.

3. USEFUL EXPRESSIONS

MATCHING   Match the responses with the questions/statements.

Question/Statement		Response
1. Hi, how may I help you?	▶ ◀	a. I'm Dave Thomas and this is Jill Foster.
2. Could you tell me your names?	▶ ◀	b. Sure. No problem.
3. Please sign here.	▶ ◀	c. It's down the hall on your left.
4. Where should we wait?	▶ ◀	d. We're here for a meeting with Kathy Gordon in Marketing.
5. Excuse me, where's the restroom?	▶ ◀	e. Over there by the magazines is fine.

11

Scene 2	MEETING COMPANY GUESTS

1. LANGUAGE NOTES

WORD BANK Fill in the blanks with the most appropriate word from the box. Change the word form wherever necessary.

currently	expect	apologize	bother	restroom

1. He _____ for the delay with the project at the meeting yesterday.

2. _____, there are 120 employees in this company.

3. The _____ on this floor are for staff only.

4. A: Sorry for the wait.   B: It's no _____ at all.

5. Our office is _____ to move to a new location next year.

PHRASES Fill in the blanks with the most appropriate phrase from the box. Change the word form wherever necessary.

my pleasure	would be great	right away	down the hall	I'm afraid

1. It's urgent. Please come to my office _____.

2. A: Thank you for your advice.   B: _____.

3. _____ that I won't be able to take the job.

4. A: Are you hungry?   B: Yeah, a snack _____.

5. A: Where's the break room?   B: It's _____.

2. VIDEO WATCHING   CHECK YOUR UNDERSTANDING

FIRST VIEWING Watch the video of Ms. Farmar's assistant, Fran, meeting with the guests at reception, and choose the correct answers.

WEB動画

1. Why can't Ms. Farmar see James and Emma now?

   A. She's got the morning off.   B. She's not at the office today.
   C. She forgot about the meeting.   D. She's in another meeting.

2. What does James say about the wait?

   A. He'll come back in the afternoon.   B. 15 minutes is the maximum he can wait.
   C. He doesn't mind waiting.   D. It is inconvenient for him and Emma.

3. What will Fran most likely do next?

   A. Make tea and coffee for everyone   B. Bring some green tea out for James
   C. Take the guests to Ms. Farmar's office   D. Tell Ms. Farmar to hurry up

12

UNIT 1 *Meeting for the First Time*

SECOND VIEWING   Watch the video again and fill in the blanks.

Ms. Farmar's assistant, Fran, comes out to meet the guests.

Fran: Hello, you must be James and Emma?

James: Yes, that's us. ① _____ Ms. Farmar.

Fran: I'm afraid Ms. Farmar is currently in another meeting, which is taking longer than expected. She apologizes for the wait. I'm her assistant, Fran.

James: It's OK. We've got the whole morning off, so it's no bother.

Fran: She ② _____ 15 minutes. Can I get you some tea or coffee while you wait?

Emma: I'm fine, thanks. I ③ _____.

James: A green tea would be great, if you have it. Thanks.

Fran: My pleasure. ④ _____ right away. Please let me know if you need anything else.

Emma: Oh, where's the restroom?

Fran: ⑤ _____, last door on the left.

3. USEFUL EXPRESSIONS

SHADOWING   Listen to the audio and practice saying the sentences below.

Explaining that someone is late	
She's (currently) in another meeting	which is taking longer than expected. and won't be available for a while.
She shouldn't be	more than 15 minutes. too long.
She's running (a bit) late	because of traffic. due to an emergency.

Language Practice

Work with a partner. Make a short conversation between an office visitor and a receptionist and fill out the visitor pass.

Sample Conversation	
Receptionist:	Hello. How can I help you?
Visitor:	Hello. I have an appointment with *(Mr. Truman)* at *(3 p.m)*.
Receptionist:	*(Ask the visitor for his/her name.)*
Visitor:	Yes, I'm *(name)* from *(company)*.
Receptionist:	*(Ask the visitor to complete the visitor pass.)*
Visitor:	OK. Here you are.
Receptionist:	All right. Let me take you to *(Mr. Truman)*.

VISITOR PASS

NAME :

COMPANY :

REASON FOR VISIT :

APPOINTMENT :

TIME IN :   TIME OUT :

DATE :

Language Function — Giving bad news / Apologizing

I'm sorry, but S+V

I'm afraid / I'm sorry / I apologize (that) + S+V

- I'm sorry, but I'll be a little late for the meeting. The traffic on the highway is very heavy this morning.
- I'm afraid our computer is down now. I apologize for / I'm sorry for the inconvenience.

Write your own apology in the following situations and explain the reasons.

1. You need to change the date and time of an appointment with your client.

   _____

2. You need to cancel an appointment with your dentist.

UNIT 1 *Meeting for the First Time*

Reading Comprehension

Read the following passage and choose **T** if the statement is true, or **F** if it is false. 1-05

When you think about business English, you probably picture scenes of executive meetings, formal presentations, and important negotiations. However, the English we use in business situations is not always formal, and is not always connected to business. Of course, managers and executives discuss contract details, marketing campaigns, and financial decisions, but they also spend time enjoying small talk, even in business situations.

Business small talk may sometimes be seen as simply a way of filling time before a meeting begins, but in reality, it is far more important than that. Success in business depends on many things, and one of these is building good relationships with colleagues and business partners. Engaging in small talk is one of the best ways to do this.

The topic of these casual conversations is not so important (although there are certainly topics, such as politics or physical appearance, that we should avoid!), but through small talk, business people can relax, get to know each other, and establish trust. When people feel comfortable with each other, they are more likely to cooperate, and this helps business discussions and negotiations to proceed successfully. Despite its name, small talk has a big role.

1. Only formal English should be used in business situations.   T☐   F☐
2. Business people often use small talk when discussing contract details.   T☐   F☐
3. Small talk helps business people to create better relationships.   T☐   F☐
4. It's OK to talk about whatever topic you like during small talk.   T☐   F☐
5. Cooperation and trust are important to success in business.   T☐   F☐

Active Learning

Task 1

Make a business card with the name of a real or imaginary company, your name, your position, and your contact information. Exchange business cards and make small talk with a partner.

Task 2

You're running late for a 10 o'clock meeting with Dan Carter of Samberg Group. Send a text message and explain the reason, as well as the expected time you'll arrive at his office. Use the expressions, "I'm sorry 〜," "I'm afraid 〜," "I apologize that 〜," or "I apologize for 〜."

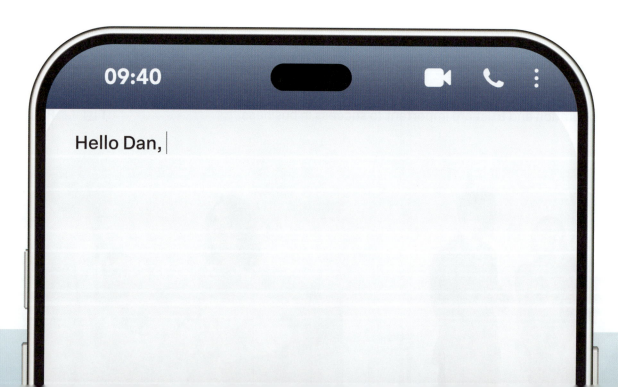

UNIT 2
Welcoming a Newcomer

Checklist

In this unit, you will learn about...
- Introducing your work environment
- Informing someone of company rules

Warm-up

List some things you can do to make newcomers feel welcome. Write the letters (A-H) in the correct box, "Before the first day" or "On the first day", depending on when they happen (some actions could be both before and on the first day). Discuss your reasons with a partner.

A. Introduce the newcomer to coworkers.

B. Connect the newcomer to online resources. (e.g. useful websites, team chat groups, social media pages)

C. Set up a desk or a new workstation.

D. Assign a team member to guide the newcomer through important tasks.

E. Tell the newcomer about company rules/policies.

F. Give the newcomer a welcome note/card or Post-it note.

G. Show the newcomer around the office.

H. Send out a welcome e-mail.

Before the first day	On the first day

Scene 1 — WORK ENVIRONMENT AND FACILITIES

1. LANGUAGE NOTES

WORD BANK Match the following words with their definitions.

1. equipment
2. supply (v)
3. employee
4. employer
5. break room

a. the necessary tools or items for a particular purpose
b. someone who is paid to work for someone else
c. to provide, to make something available to someone
d. a place at a company where you eat lunch, drink coffee, etc.
e. a person or company that gives work to someone

PHRASES Fill in the blanks with the most appropriate phrase from the box. Change the word form wherever necessary.

| go on a tour | run out of | such as | help yourself | what if |

1. Lisa _____ time and didn't finish the report.
2. You should eat healthy food, _____ vegetables and fish.
3. I know it's convenient, but _____ I don't like to use online banking? How can I pay for it?
4. I _____ of the office yesterday before starting work.
5. Please _____ to more drinks if you like.

2. VIDEO WATCHING — CHECK YOUR UNDERSTANDING

FIRST VIEWING Watch the video of Ryan showing Janice a new workplace, and choose the correct answers.

1. What can Janice do if she needs more supplies?
   A. She can get more from the cabinet behind Lisa's desk.
   B. She can go into the break room to get more.
   C. She can find them in the room at the back of the office.
   D. She can go buy her own supplies from the shop next door.

2. Where is the water cooler?
   A. Next to the supply cabinet
   B. In the room at the back of the office
   C. In the room with the coffee maker
   D. By Lisa's desk

3. What is in the room at the back of the office?
   A. The water cooler and coffee maker
   B. Lisa's desk
   C. The copier and printer
   D. Pens and notepads

18

UNIT 2 *Welcoming a Newcomer*

SECOND VIEWING
Watch the video again and fill in the blanks with the words below.

  1-06

| something to drink | at the back of | the supply cabinet |
| in the break room | run out of supplies | |

Janice goes with Ryan on a tour of the workplace.

Ryan: So, Janice, this is your desk.

Janice: OK.

Ryan: If you ①_____, like pens and notepads, you can help yourself to more from ②_____. It's in the corner there behind Lisa's desk.

Janice: All right. What if I need ③_____? Is there a water cooler in here?

Ryan: Yes. Actually, we have a water cooler and coffee maker available for employees ④_____. That's the first door on your left after you enter the office.

Janice: Oh, I think I went in there earlier.

Ryan: All of the equipment you'll need for work, such as the copier and printer, are in the room here ⑤_____ the office.

Janice: I see.

Ryan: I think that's all of the important things. Do you have any questions?

Janice: Not yet, but if I have a problem, I'll let you know.

3. USEFUL EXPRESSIONS

SHADOWING
The word "supply" can be used in different ways. Listen to the audio and practice saying the sentences below.

 1-07

Usage	Example Sentence
a **supply** of + N	There is usually a good **supply** of paper next to the photocopier.
supplies	We needed to buy more cleaning **supplies** for the office.
in short **supply**	We've all been working overtime this week, so coffee is now in short **supply**.
supply somebody with + N	The office **supplied** all the employees with cell phones.
supplied by somebody	Our computers were **supplied** by the company.

19

Scene 2 — THE COMPANY'S RULES

1. LANGUAGE NOTES

WORD BANK Fill in the blanks with the most appropriate word from the box. Change the word form wherever necessary.

explain	policy	wave	rule	scanner

1. Linda _____ when she saw her coworker enter the room.
2. The _____ is broken, so you can't use it today.
3. It's our _____ to allow employees to wear casual clothes on Fridays.
4. Tyron _____ the schedule to me at the last meeting.
5. The most important _____ is to be on time for work.

PHRASES Fill in the blanks with the most appropriate phrase from the box. Change the word form wherever necessary.

lunch break	clock in	clock out	keep ~ on	turn off

1. Make sure that you _____ the lights when you leave the office.
2. Louise is the last person to take a _____ every day.
3. Before you _____, please see your boss.
4. Please remember that you must _____ your ID badge _____ at work.
5. Paige forgot to _____ yesterday morning.

2. VIDEO WATCHING — CHECK YOUR UNDERSTANDING

FIRST VIEWING Watch the video of Ryan explaining some office rules to Janice, and choose the correct answers.

1. What do employees need to wear in the office?
   - A. A business card
   - B. A scanner
   - C. A security badge
   - D. An ID badge

2. How can employees clock in?
   - A. They need to talk to Wendell about it.
   - B. They need to wave their badge in front of a scanner.
   - C. They need to put on their IDs.
   - D. They need to clock in before 9 a.m.

3. When can employees take a lunch break?
   - A. They can leave after they clock out.
   - B. They need to ask Wendell when it is OK.
   - C. They can go when they are hungry.
   - D. They are allowed to go before clocking in.

UNIT 2 *Welcoming a Newcomer*

SECOND VIEWING   Watch the video again and fill in the blanks.   1-08

Ryan explains some of the rules of the office to Janice.

Ryan: Janice, have you been given ①_____ yet?

Janice: Yes, Wendell gave it to me this morning.

Ryan: Great. It is company policy to wear your badge while in the office. So you need to ②_____.

Janice: No problem.

Ryan: Also, when you come in and leave every day, you need to ③_____ in front of the scanner by the front door.

Janice: Right. Wendell helped me with that this morning.

Ryan: Good. Please remember that you must ④_____ a.m., and you can't clock out until 5 p.m., or you will lose some of your pay.

Janice: I understand. What about lunch?

Ryan: You can take a one-hour lunch break ⑤_____. You don't need to clock in or out for it.

Janice: OK. Thanks for all your help.

3. USEFUL EXPRESSIONS

SEQUENCING   Number the statements in a natural order to make a conversation. Listen to the audio to check your answer. 1-09

_____	I just wave my ID in front of the scanner, right?
_____	Please do.
_____	That's right. You'll do the same thing to clock out at 5 p.m.
_____	First, remember to clock in by 9 a.m.
_____	I'd like to talk to you about our company's policies.

21

Language Practice

Work with a partner. You are a new employee at a company.
Ask your coworker for more details about the company policies.

New employee:	Do we need to wear an ID badge at our workplace?
Coworker:	
New employee:	What time do we need to clock in and out?
Coworker:	
New employee:	How long is the lunch break? When do we need to go and come back?
Coworker:	

Ask a few more questions.
(e.g. paid vacation policy, travel expenses, housing allowance, benefits, etc.)

New employee:	Do we need to wear an ID badge at our workplace?
Coworker:	
New employee:	What time do we need to clock in and out?
Coworker:	

Language Function — Giving advice / instructions

Imperative + and + S	Imperative + or + S + V
→ Positive results	→ Negative results

1. **Do these sentences show a positive result or a negative result?**

Advice / instruction	Result	
A. Restart your computer, and <u>that might fix the problem</u>.		positive / negative
B. Turn off the lights when you leave, or <u>it will waste energy</u>.		positive / negative
C. Listen carefully, or <u>you won't understand what to do</u>.		positive / negative
D. Type the following code, and <u>you can reset the password</u>.		positive / negative

2. **Write your own sentences using this pattern.**

A. _____

B. _____

C. _____

UNIT 2 *Welcoming a Newcomer*

Reading Comprehension

Read the following passage and choose the correct answer.

 1-10

    For many workers, such as police officers, wearing a set uniform is a requirement of their job. In the business world, a different type of uniform is common. Take a look around a busy train carriage in rush hour, and you will probably see half the passengers dressed in "office wear," a formal suit which is seen as a kind of uniform in many workplaces.

    However, some people feel that having to wear the same type of clothing to work every day is a hassle. In the modern world, especially when so much business now takes place online, this dress code may seem old-fashioned. But think of some of the world's most successful entrepreneurs and what they wear. Mark Zuckerberg is famous for dressing in an identical gray T-shirt every day, and Steve Jobs wore nothing but black turtle-necks for years. This too is a type of informal uniform.

    Busy people need to save every minute they can, and choosing what to wear each morning takes time and effort. Whether your job has a set uniform, traditional office wear, or a more modern alternative, having some kind of dress code means one less decision you need to make every day!

1. How many types of uniforms are mentioned?
       A. One   B. Two   C. Three   D. Four

2. What disadvantage of office wear is mentioned?
       A. It makes workers look too formal.
       B. It's more uncomfortable than casual clothes.
       C. It's not suited to the modern world.
       D. It stops people from expressing their own fashion sense.

3. What advantage of having a workplace dress code is mentioned?
       A. All employees feel equal.
       B. All employees look professional.
       C. You can save money on clothes.
       D. You can save time in the morning.

Active Learning

Task 1

Read the list of policies at ABC Ltd. Then, write three policies you would like to have if you started your own company and explain why.

Company policies at ABC Ltd.

1. Our flextime policy allows employees to work seven hours between 8 a.m. and 8 p.m. excluding the lunch break.

2. Employees can work remotely some days, but they are required to come into the office three days a week.

3. Twenty days of paid holiday per year are permitted, but should be booked in advance.

Company policies at *your company*

1.

2.

3.

Task 2

You are new at work. Ask your coworker the locations of some departments in the company. An example of question and response is given below. Write down two more questions and answers before you and a partner do the role play.

Newcomer: Hello **_Janice_**, I need some help with finding my way around. Can you tell me where **_the Personnel Department_** is?

Coworker: It's in room 7 on the second floor.

Newcomer: _____?

Coworker: _____.

Newcomer: _____?

Coworker: _____.

Newcomer: Thanks a lot. I hope I'll figure out where things are in the building soon.

Departments

HR (Human Resources)/Personnel
2nd Floor Room 7

IT (Information Technology)
3rd Floor Room 3

PR (Public Relations)
1st Floor Room 5

Customer Service
the second room on your left

R & D (Research and Development)
4th Floor, the whole floor

Administration Office
the first room on your right

Sales
down the hall

UNIT 3
Telephone Communication

✓ Checklist
In this unit, you will learn about...
- Answering the phone and connecting a caller
- Rescheduling a meeting time

Warm-up

Which types of communication do you use the most?
(Write 4 = Very often, 3 = Often, 2 = Sometimes, 1 = Seldom, 0 = Never)
Tell a partner about how often and in what situations you do these things.

☐ use a landline phone (office / home)

☐ make a voice call (cellphone)

☐ make a voice call (app)

☐ have a text chat

☐ have a video chat

☐ use a payphone

Scene 1 — INCOMING CALLS

1. LANGUAGE NOTES

WORD BANK — Match the following words with their meanings.

1. corporation
2. hold
3. available
4. actually
5. sure

a. free, not busy
b. to be honest, in fact
c. to wait on the telephone
d. OK, no problem
e. company, business

PHRASES — Fill in the blanks with the most appropriate phrase from the box. Change the word form wherever necessary.

| in about an hour | at the moment | call back | put you through | this is ~ speaking |

1. The secretary will _____ to the manager.
2. Hannah will _____ later this afternoon.
3. Tom is not in the office _____.
4. Parlow Corporation. _____ Liz _____. May I help you?
5. His phone is busy now, so I'll try again _____.

2. VIDEO WATCHING — CHECK YOUR UNDERSTANDING

FIRST VIEWING — Watch the video of Hannah answering the calls coming in to the office, and choose the correct answers.

1. Why does Hannah ask the first caller, John, to hold?
   A. The man John wants to talk to isn't there.
   B. She needs to check if Matt is free.
   C. She doesn't know who John wants to talk to.
   D. There isn't anyone in Matt's office.

2. Who was put through to Matt?
   A. Sam
   B. Hannah
   C. John
   D. Matt

3. What will the second caller, Sam, do?
   A. He'll find Matt in his office.
   B. He'll wait for a moment.
   C. He'll call again later.
   D. He'll talk to Matt now.

UNIT 3 *Telephone Communication*

SECOND VIEWING
Watch the video again and fill in the blanks with the words below.

  1-11

| Can you call back later | How can I help you | I'll put you through |
| I don't have much time | I need to talk to him | |

Hannah is answering calls coming into the office.

Hannah: Harlow Corporation, Mr. Horner's office, Hannah speaking.
① _____ ?

John: Good morning, Hannah. My name is John Umber. I need to speak to Matt Horner.

Hannah: OK, Mr. Umber. Please hold. I'll see if he's available.

John: Thank you very much. *(Hannah checks if Matt Horner is available.)*

Hannah: All right, Mr. Umber. ② _____ to Mr. Horner.

John: Thanks. *(The phone rings again.)*

Hannah: Harlow Corporation, Mr. Horner's office. This is Hannah speaking. Can I help you?

Sam: Hello. This is Sam Jackson. Is Matt available?
③ _____ .

Hannah: I'm sorry. His line's busy at the moment. Can you hold?

Sam: Actually, ④ _____ to wait right now.

Hannah: I do apologize, but I'm afraid Mr. Horner is not available at the moment. ⑤ _____ ?

Sam: Sure. I'll try again in about an hour.

3. USEFUL EXPRESSIONS

MATCHING
Match the responses with the questions/statements.

Question/Statement		Response
1. Hello. How can I help you?	▶ ◀	a. OK.
2. Let me check if she is free.	▶ ◀	b. Actually, I don't have much time now. I'll call back in the afternoon.
3. Jenny's line is busy at the moment. Can you hold?	▶ ◀	c. Thank you. You, too.
4. All right. Have a nice day.	▶ ◀	d. I need to speak to Jenny Taylor. Is she available?

| Scene 2 | RESCHEDULING AN APPOINTMENT |

1. LANGUAGE NOTES

WORD BANK   Fill in the blanks with the most appropriate word from the box. Change the word form wherever necessary.

application	representative	serious	assistance	postpone

1. I can't understand this. Let's ask Rachel for _____.

2. Because two employees are sick, the meeting has been _____ until next week.

3. Steve is a _____ for Eaton Books. He travels around the city telling people about the company.

4. It says on your _____ that you have previous experience with two companies.

5. Doctors said her condition was _____ but stable.

PHRASES   Fill in the blanks with the most appropriate phrase from the box. Change the word form wherever necessary.

apply for	look for	come up	check with	get back to

1. It's best to _____ as many jobs as possible in order to give yourself more choices.

2. I'm busy right now. Do you mind if I _____ you after lunch?

3. I'm sorry. I planned to go to your party, but something else _____.

4. I'm _____ Victoria. Do you know where she is?

5. That looks correct, but can you _____ Mike just to make sure?

2. VIDEO WATCHING   CHECK YOUR UNDERSTANDING

FIRST VIEWING   Watch the video of Angela calling a company about a job she has applied for, and choose the correct answers.

1. What is Peter Jones doing at the moment?

    A. Having a job interview
    B. Taking a business trip
    C. Going to the hospital
    D. Going on a vacation

2. Why does Angela need to reschedule with Mr. Jones?

    A. She has another interview.
    B. She'll be out of town.
    C. She needs to go to the hospital.
    D. She'll visit someone at the hospital.

3. What will the man do next?

    A. Apply for the position of sales representative.

    B. Go on a business trip until tomorrow afternoon.

    C. Cancel Mr. Jones's appointment for next Friday.

    D. Ask Peter Jones if it is OK to postpone the interview.

UNIT 3 *Telephone Communication*

SECOND VIEWING Watch the video again and fill in the blanks.

Angela is calling a company about a job she has applied for.

Angela: Hi, my name is Angela Stokes, and I'm looking for a Mr. Peter Jones.

Julio: I'm afraid Mr. Jones is out of the office.

Angela: I'm calling about my application for ①_____.
He had asked me to come in for an interview next Tuesday.

Julio: Oh, yes. Tuesday at 4 p.m., right?

Angela: Yes. I e-mailed him but ②_____. Do you know when he'll be back?

Julio: He's currently on a business trip until tomorrow afternoon. If you need assistance, I can help.

Angela: Well, something's come up, and I have to ③_____ for a few days.

Julio: Oh, nothing too serious?

Angela: It's fine, thanks. But I was wondering if we could ④_____ until Thursday or Friday?

Julio: I'll have to check with Peter on that. I can pass your LINE on to him and ⑤_____ as soon as he can.

Angela: Sure. My LINE ID is angelayang456. Thanks.

3. USEFUL EXPRESSIONS

FILLING IN THE BLANKS Complete each sentence with the most appropriate phrase from the box.

Hold on	Could you wait	Who's calling	May I speak to

	Formal	Semi-Formal	Informal
Making a call	1._____ Jenny?	Can I talk to Jenny, please?	Is Jenny there?
Asking who is calling	Could you tell me who is calling, please?	3._____, please?	Who's this?
Asking someone to hold	2._____ just a moment, please?	Just a moment, please.	Just a second. Just a moment. 4._____.

29

Language Practice

Work with a partner and practice the sample phone conversation between a member of staff and a client. Then create your own conversation, changing the underlined expressions.

Staff:	Good afternoon, <u>Danny speaking</u>. How can I help you?
Client:	Hello. This is <u>Celia Walters from Harris Industries</u>. I'm trying to reach <u>Shelly Turner in Marketing</u>.
Staff:	I'm sorry. <u>Ms. Turner is away from her desk</u> at the moment. Can I take a message?
Client:	Sure. Please tell her that I need her to call me back. She can reach me <u>at 585-3641 until six o'clock</u>.
Staff:	Let me repeat that. She can call you <u>at 585-3641, but only before six</u>.
Client:	That's right. Thank you.

Language Function — Making polite requests

I was wondering if + S + could + V

- *I was wondering if* I could borrow your book on office design. I'd like to get some ideas.
- *I was wondering if* we could postpone our meeting till next Monday. I have a fever now.

Write your own requests in the following situations and explain the reasons.

1. You want to borrow a book on Europe from your friend.

2. You want the staff at a furniture store to send you a new catalogue.

3. You want your colleague to teach you how to use the new design software.

4. You want your colleague to give you a ride to work next Friday.

UNIT 3 Telephone Communication

Reading Comprehension

Read the following passage and choose **T** if the statement is true, or **F** if it is false. 1-13

In recent years, technology has transformed communication in the business world and beyond. Many conversations which previously happened on the telephone now take place via email, messaging apps, or video conferencing. Nevertheless, the telephone is still an important tool in our lives, and most of us now carry a phone wherever we go. However, the way telephones are used has also changed a lot.

These days, if you call a company, it is often quite hard to reach a real human being who you can talk to. Sometimes, you may be put on hold and spend a long time waiting while listening to background music. Often you may have to listen to several different voice messages and choose options from various menus before you can talk to a person. And for some services, such as parcel delivery, the whole phone call can now be automated, and you never talk to a person at all.

While these experiences may not always be enjoyable for customers, from the company's point of view, systems like these are cheaper and more efficient. It is also possible that telephone services will continue to change. Perhaps, instead of dealing with menus and recorded messages, we may one day be having live telephone conversations with AI generated voices.

1. Telephone conversations are now more important in business than ever. T☐ F☐
2. Calling a company and talking to a person is usually a quick and efficient process. T☐ F☐
3. It is now possible to complete a business phone call without speaking to anyone. T☐ F☐
4. Companies use voice message systems to help save money. T☐ F☐
5. In the future, it is likely that telephones will no longer be used to provide customer service. T☐ F☐

Active Learning

Task 1

Write the full version of each abbreviation (a short form of a word) in the box and fill in the blanks with these abbreviations. Then, read the text message aloud with a partner.

ASAP = _____   plz = _____
u = _____   thx = _____
FB = _____   NP = _____

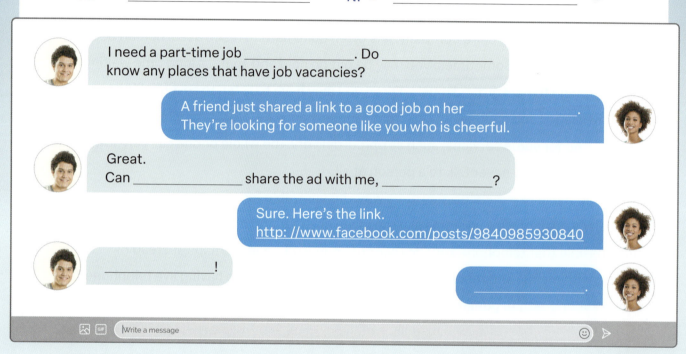

I need a part-time job _____. Do _____ know any places that have job vacancies?

A friend just shared a link to a good job on her _____. They're looking for someone like you who is cheerful.

Great. Can _____ share the ad with me, _____?

Sure. Here's the link.
http://www.facebook.com/posts/9840985930840

_____!

_____.

Task 2

Work with a partner. Call your client and leave a message with his/her secretary. The secretary fills out the phone message below. Then switch roles.

Phone Message While You Were Out

For _____   Department _____

Date _____   Time _____

Caller's Name: Maria Garcia

Caller's Company: _____

Caller's Phone#: _____

Message: _____

UNIT 4
Office Issues

Checklist

In this unit, you will learn about...
- Asking for leave
- Working overtime and covering shifts

Warm-up

Tell a partner what benefits you think a company should provide. Rank your first three choices (1-3) in order of importance. Compare your answers with a partner.

☐ Regular pay raises

☐ Overtime pay

☐ Annual bonuses

☐ Recreation

☐ Free coffee/tea/snacks

☐ Free lunches

☐ Paid time off

☐ Company trips

☐ Flexible schedules

Scene 1 — TAKING TIME OFF

1. LANGUAGE NOTES

WORD BANK — Match the following words with their definitions.

1. flu
2. appear
3. realize
4. form
5. sign

a. to come to understand, to know
b. to write one's name officially
c. to seem, to look like
d. influenza, a type of illness like a cold
e. official paper, document

PHRASES — Fill in the blanks with the most appropriate phrase from the box. Change the word form wherever necessary.

take time off	according to	sick leave	annual leave	have ~ left

1. _____ Marianne, Tom wasn't very helpful with the project.
2. Last week I took some _____ because I had a high fever.
3. This is a busy time of year, so you can't _____ next week.
4. We only _____ five days _____ before the project deadline.
5. Employees at this company can take 10 days of paid _____.

2. VIDEO WATCHING — CHECK YOUR UNDERSTANDING

FIRST VIEWING — Watch the video of Carla asking her manager, Bob, for time off work, and choose the correct answers.

1. Why did Carla take three days off last week?
   A. She went on vacation.
   B. She was sick.
   C. She went to Hong Kong.
   D. She had annual leave to use.

2. How many days does Carla have left for her vacation?
   A. Three days
   B. Five days
   C. Seven days
   D. Ten days

3. What does Carla have to do to get her days off?
   A. She needs to talk to someone else.
   B. She needs to fill out a form.
   C. She needs to get a form for Bob to sign.
   D. She needs to ask Bob again later.

UNIT 4 *Office Issues*

SECOND VIEWING Watch the video again and fill in the blanks with the words below.   1-14

| I had taken so many | I'll sign it for you | I took some sick leave |
| only have three days left | take your last three days off | |

Carla is asking her manager, Bob, for time off work.

Carla: Hey, Bob. Can I take some time off next month?

Bob: Didn't you take three days off last week?

Carla: Yes, ①_____, because I had the flu.

Bob: I see. Next month you need to take some annual leave then?

Carla: Right. I should have about five days left, and I'd like to go to Hong Kong.

Bob: Looking at your file, it appears that you ②_____.

Carla: Are you sure? We get 10 days of annual leave a year, right?

Bob: That's right. According to this, you've taken seven of your annual leave days.

Carla: I didn't realize that ③_____.

Bob: Do you still want to ④_____ next month?

Carla: Yes, please.

Bob: OK. Go get the form, and ⑤_____.

3. USEFUL EXPRESSIONS

SHADOWING Listen to the audio and practice saying the sentences below. 1-15

Taking Leave

1. I need to **take leave** for a few days.
2. I **am taking some time off** for a few days.
3. I haven't used all of my **paid vacation days**.
4. Can I **apply for my annual leave**?
5. When would be a good time for me to **take a vacation**?
6. Would it be possible for me to **take paid leave**?

35

Scene 2 ▶ FINDING A REPLACEMENT

1. LANGUAGE NOTES

WORD BANK — Fill in the blanks with the most appropriate word from the box. Change the word form wherever necessary.

raise	shift	rate	comp	instead

1. Our regular _____ is US $12 an hour.
2. Richard didn't call his client but wrote an email to her _____.
3. Everyone in the office received a pay _____ last month.
4. I have a lot of _____ time saved up that I'm going to use next month.
5. I need someone to cover my _____ next Friday because I have a wedding to attend.

PHRASES — Fill in the blanks with the most appropriate phrase from the box. Change the word form wherever necessary.

overtime pay	on vacation	take a trip	allowed to	let me know

1. I'm going to _____ to Vietnam with my friends next week.
2. Workers are _____ take an hour lunch break.
3. Now the project is over, and I'll be _____ all this week.
4. When you finish writing the report, please _____.
5. Employees are demanding the company give them _____.

2. VIDEO WATCHING — CHECK YOUR UNDERSTANDING

FIRST VIEWING — Watch the video of Bob asking Sarah to cover Carla's shifts while Carla is on vacation. Answer **T** (true) or **F** (false) based on the conversation.

1. Sarah will cover two shifts for Carla. T☐ F☐
2. Sarah will receive overtime pay. T☐ F☐
3. Overtime pay is twice the regular rate at the company. T☐ F☐
4. Sarah knows which days she wants to take off. T☐ F☐

36

UNIT 4 *Office Issues*

SECOND VIEWING Watch the video again and fill in the blanks.   1-16

Bob is asking one of his employees, Sarah, to cover Carla's shifts while Carla is on vacation.

Bob: Sarah, do you ①_____ for the 15th and 16th of next month?

Sarah: No. Why?

Bob: Carla is taking a trip, and I need someone to ②_____.

Sarah: What days of the week are the 15th and 16th?

Bob: It's a Saturday and Sunday.

Sarah: I guess I could do it. Will I receive overtime pay? It's still 1.5 times my regular rate, right?

Bob: Sorry, but ③_____ give overtime pay for covering shifts anymore. You'll receive comp time instead.

Sarah: I guess having a few days off with pay would be OK.

Bob: Do you know what days you'd like to ④_____?

Sarah: Can I tell you later? I'm not sure.

Bob: That's fine. Just ⑤_____ by the end of the week. Thanks for your help.

3. USEFUL EXPRESSIONS

SEQUENCING Number the statements in a natural order to make a conversation. Listen to the audio to check your answer. 1-17

____	Hmm. Let me check my schedule. Let's see... Sorry Ava, I'm working Friday morning already.
____	Amy covered a shift for me last week, and she said she won't do it again.
____	Oh, no! What am I going to do? I have a doctor's appointment that day.
____	Hey, Ron. Would you be able to cover a shift for me on Friday?
____	How about asking Amy? I don't think she's working on Friday.

37

Language Practice

Work with a partner and practice the sample phone conversation between an employee and a manager. Then create your own conversation, changing the underlined expressions.

Employee:	Hi, Mitch. I want to talk to you about taking some leave.
Manager:	OK. When do you need time off?
Employee:	I need to take leave from May 14th to May 18th.
Manager:	Why do you need to take so many vacation days?
Employee:	Actually, it's my mother's birthday on the 16th. I want to go home and surprise her.
Manager:	I see. I'll try to find someone to cover your work while you're away.
Employee:	Thank you. I appreciate it. I'll be back on the 21st.

Language Function — Explaining restrictions / regulations

~ be allowed to + V (infinitive)

- **You're allowed to** ask questions anytime during the meeting tomorrow.
- **Employees are not allowed to** work remotely anymore.

Write your own sentences, using either "allowed to" or "not allowed to" and add a further comment.

1. (⭕ wear casual clothes in the office on Fridays)

   _____

2. (❌ take sales data back home)

   _____

3. (⭕ eat lunch for free at our company cafeteria)

   _____

4. (❌ smoke anywhere inside the office building)

   _____

UNIT 4 *Office Issues*

Reading Comprehension

Read the following passage and choose the correct answer.

 1-18

The number of days of paid annual leave that companies offer their employees can vary considerably. In most countries, a minimum number of days is decided by law. In Europe, workers usually have the right to take at least 20 days of paid holiday per year. This is also true in many countries in Africa and Asia.

In the USA, on the other hand, there is no law requiring companies to offer any paid vacation. In practice, most companies do offer around 10 days, but even this is quite low compared to much of the world. American workers may get many benefits, but long paid vacations are not one of them.

However, the number of days required by law is not the only important factor. In Japan, for example, companies give 10 to 20 days of paid leave, depending on how long employees have worked, but many people do not take their full number of days. It is also very rare for someone to take a week or two of paid leave at one time, which is normal in Europe. This is because Japanese workers often worry that their coworkers will have to work harder if they take leave. It seems that employment benefits are affected not only by law, but also by culture.

1. Why do companies in many parts of the world allow their employees paid vacation days?
   A. It is required by law.
   B. It helps them recruit better workers.
   C. People work harder if they have a vacation to look forward to.
   D. All of these reasons.

2. How many days of paid annual leave do companies in the USA have to offer their staff?
   A. None   B. Five   C. Ten   D. Twenty

3. Why don't Japanese employees often take one to two weeks of paid leave?
   A. Their companies do not allow it.
   B. They worry that their bosses will be angry if they do.
   C. Japanese law does not set a minimum number of days.
   D. They are concerned about the effect on other staff members.

Active Learning

Task 1

Research one company you are interested in and find out about the benefits they provide employees. Then, make a four-page slideshow explaining about the company and their benefits.

Slide 1 - Company Information
(Company Name, Year of Establishment, CEO, Products/Services)

Slide 2 - Unique Characteristics

Slide 3 - Benefits

Slide 4 - Benefits

Company Information	Unique Characteristics

Benefits	Benefits

Task 2

Based on the information you obtain on the company and slides you create, make a 4-minute presentation.

UNIT 5

Arranging a Meeting

Checklist

In this unit, you will learn about...

- Planning a meeting
- Reserving a meeting space and supplies

Warm-up

Match the names of the meeting room items with the pictures.
What other things are needed for meetings? Discuss with a partner.

☐ digital projector

☐ projection screen

☐ laptop

☐ extension cord

☐ laser pointer

☐ speakers

☐ whiteboard

☐ marker

☐ whiteboard eraser

A

B

C

D

E

F

G

H

I

Scene 1 — MEETING PREPARATIONS

1. LANGUAGE NOTES

WORD BANK — Match the following words with their meanings.

1. arrange
2. branch
3. usually
4. rent
5. conference

a. large meeting, convention
b. to prepare for
c. smaller office or store, local office or store
d. normally, generally
e. to lease, to pay to use something for a fixed time

PHRASES — Fill in the blanks with the most appropriate phrase from the box. Change the word form wherever necessary.

| keep that the same   find out   would you like to   make sure   sounds good |

1. Please contact the clients and _____ how many are coming tomorrow.
2. We need to _____ we have enough chairs for the participants.
3. A: Is this Friday okay with you? B: _____ to me.
4. The event usually takes place in May, so let's _____.
5. Where _____ have the next meeting?

2. VIDEO WATCHING — CHECK YOUR UNDERSTANDING

FIRST VIEWING — Watch the video of Lisa asking her assistant, Michael, to help her arrange a meeting, and choose the correct answers.

WEB動画

1. When will the meeting be held?
   A. On a Friday in May
   B. On a Friday in March
   C. On a Saturday in May
   D. On a Saturday in March

2. Who will come to the meeting?
   A. Only managers
   B. The company's top salespeople
   C. All of the people who work at Lisa's branch
   D. Sales managers and some salespeople

3. Why does Michael need to contact the sales managers?
   A. To know how many salespeople they will bring
   B. To find out if they want to come to the meeting
   C. To ask which branch they work at
   D. To let them know that the meeting will happen

UNIT 5 *Arranging a Meeting*

SECOND VIEWING
Watch the video again and fill in the blanks with the words below.

The sales manager from every branch	we rented a conference room
What time would you like	When would you like to have	Which date in March

Lisa asks her assistant, Michael, to help her arrange a meeting.

Lisa: Michael, I need you to help me arrange our company's annual sales meeting this year.

Michael: I'm happy to help. ① _____ the meeting?

Lisa: It usually happens in March, so let's keep that the same.

Michael: OK. ② _____ would be good?

Lisa: Any Friday should be fine.

Michael: ③ _____ to start?

Lisa: Anytime. Just make sure we can finish everything by 6 p.m.

Michael: All right. And who will be coming to the meeting?

Lisa: ④ _____ will come. They will each bring their top salespeople. You'll need to contact them and find out how many they each will be bringing.

Michael: I'll e-mail them right away. Where would you like to hold the meeting?

Lisa: Last year, ⑤ _____ at the Windom Hotel. Let's do that again.

Michael: Sounds good.

3. USEFUL EXPRESSIONS

MATCHING
Match the responses with the questions/statements.

Question/Statement	Response
1. When would you like to hold the event?	a. Sure. I'd be happy to help.
2. Could you help me arrange an office party?	b. There's nothing available here right now.
3. Where should we have the meeting?	c. Every employee is allowed to come, and they can bring their families.
4. Who will be coming to the company's annual Christmas party?	d. I think that we should have it next month.
5. Can we rent some more office space in this building?	e. Can we hold it in our main office?

43

| Scene 2 | MAKING ARRANGEMENTS |

1. LANGUAGE NOTES

WORD BANK Fill in the blanks with the most appropriate word from the box. Change the word form wherever necessary.

reserve	projector	cordless	refreshments	serve

1. Do you know how this _____ lamp works?

2. We _____ a table for five at the new restaurant downtown yesterday.

3. Always _____ your guests their meals first at the dinner table.

4. No one seems to know how to use the _____.

5. There will be plenty of _____ during the break.

PHRASES Fill in the blanks with the most appropriate phrase from the box. Change the word form wherever necessary.

set up	on that day	would you mind	all set	repeat back

1. Can you _____ the computer for me?

2. _____ opening the window? We need some fresh air.

3. I'm afraid we don't have a room available _____.

4. Thank you for your order. Let me _____ what you said.

5. We are _____ for the presentation this Friday.

2. VIDEO WATCHING CHECK YOUR UNDERSTANDING

FIRST VIEWING Watch the video of Michael calling the Windom Hotel to reserve a conference room, and choose the correct answers.

WEB動画

1. What does Michael want to do?

   A. He wants to reserve a hotel room to stay in.   B. He wants to order food for everyone.

   C. He wants to reserve a conference room.   D. He wants to attend a meeting at the hotel.

2. How many people will come to the event?

   A. 11   B. 21   C. 93   D. 100

3. What does Michael need in the room?

   A. He needs a projector, cordless microphones, and refreshments.

   B. He needs a monitor, cordless microphones, and laptops.

   C. He needs a projector, laptops, and refreshments.

   D. He needs a monitor, cordless microphones, and refreshments.

UNIT 5 *Arranging a Meeting*

SECOND VIEWING Watch the video again and fill in the blanks.

Michael is calling the Windom Hotel to reserve a conference room.

Receptionist: Thank you for calling the Windom Hotel. How may I help you?

Michael: Hello. I would like to reserve a conference room for a meeting on ①_____, _____ at 11:00 in the morning. We need a room for 93 people.

Receptionist: OK, sir. We do have a room available on that day.

Michael: Does the room ②_____?

Receptionist: We can set one up for you.

Michael: Could you also ③_____?

Receptionist: Sure. Will you need any refreshments?

Michael: Yes. We'll need sandwiches, salad, and fruit to eat, and some ④_____.

Receptionist: All right. We can provide that for you. Your reservation is all set.

Michael: Would you mind repeating that back to me?

Receptionist: You have reserved a conference room on March 21st at 11:00 for 93 people. You need a projector and cordless microphones. ⑤_____.

Michael: Perfect. Thank you.

3. USEFUL EXPRESSIONS

FILLING IN THE BLANKS Complete each sentence with the most appropriate phrase from the box.

| a change to the system | sales experience | each branch | the most new business |

A. Sales totals from _____ were reported.

B. John Swift gave a presentation about his _____.

C. Annie Twins was named as the salesperson who brought in _____.

D. Announcements were made about _____ the company uses to report sales.

45

Language Practice

Work with a partner and practice the sample phone conversation between event staff and hotel staff. Then create your own conversation, changing the underlined expressions.

Event Staff:	I'd like to reserve a conference room for <u>100 people next Wednesday</u>.
Hotel Staff:	OK, sir / ma'am. We do <u>have a room available</u> on that day.
Event Staff:	Great. Could you <u>provide a microphone and projector</u> as well?
Hotel Staff:	No problem. We can <u>set those up</u> for you.
Event Staff:	Thanks. I also need <u>refreshments for my guests</u>.
Hotel Staff:	We'll have <u>sandwiches, tea, and coffee</u> available for everyone.
Event Staff:	<u>That sounds good</u>. Thank you.

Language Function — Making polite requests

Would you mind + V ing

- **Would you mind** open**ing** the window? It's stuffy in here.
- **Would you mind** say**ing** that again? I couldn't hear well.

Write your own request in the following situations and explain the reasons.

1. Ask your client if you can change the time of the meeting.

   _____

2. Ask the hotel staff to turn on the air conditioner in the party room.

   _____

3. Ask the staff at a restaurant to turn down the music.

   _____

4. Ask the staff at a conference hall to give you a price list for both big and small rooms.

   _____

Reading Comprehension

Read the following passage and choose **T** if the statement is true, or **F** if it is false.

> For large global companies, holding meetings involving people from different branches in different countries is a regular occurrence. However, when people from various countries participate in meetings together, cultural differences may affect their interactions.
>
> In some countries, such as Japan, meetings tend to be organized quite formally, even between people who work together all the time. Usually, there will be a written agenda which is followed strictly. People will speak in turn, and very rarely interrupt each other, which would be considered rude. Direct disagreement is also unusual for the same reason.
>
> In contrast, meeting etiquette in some other countries is much more relaxed. For example, in Britain it is not unusual to go off topic and talk about issues that are not on the agenda. Interrupting other speakers is very common, and if you wait for "your turn" to speak, you may never get the chance! Nobody will be offended if you disagree with their opinions, and in general most people prefer to speak frankly. Neither of these styles is better or worse than the other. However, when people from different countries are attending a meeting, the person in charge needs to be aware of cultural differences and try to deal sensitively with any misunderstandings.

1. Companies with many international branches tend to avoid holding meetings.   T☐ F☐
2. Business meetings in Britain are usually more formal than in Japan.   T☐ F☐
3. Interrupting when another person is speaking is considered rude in both Japan and Britain.   T☐ F☐
4. Organizing meetings in a formal way is better than the more relaxed style.   T☐ F☐
5. It is important to consider cultural differences when organizing and leading international meetings.   T☐ F☐

Active Learning

Task 1

You and your colleague are preparing for a seminar on business leadership that is going to be held with a guest speaker tomorrow afternoon. Chat with each other and finalize what needs to be done before the event.

[Ask B to bring the laptop to Room 18 tomorrow.]

[Tell A that you will. Ask A where you can find the extension cord.]

[Tell B where the extension cord is.]

[Tell A you will look for it. Ask A who is introducing the guest speaker.]

[Tell B that you will. Ask B to give you the guest speaker's bio by email.]

[Tell A that you will do that right away.]

[Thank B. Tell B that you will double-check everything tomorrow morning.]

Task 2

You have been asked to create a flyer about the business leadership seminar. Include the necessary information, add related visual images, and make a flyer. Here is some information you may want to include in the flyer.

- the name of the seminar
- the date and time
- the purpose of the seminar
- the name of the guest speaker
- the admission fees (or free admission)
- the after party

UNIT 6
Video Conferencing

✓ Checklist
In this unit, you will learn about...
- Making video calls
- Dealing with problems

Warm-up

Decide which of the following are advantages or disadvantages of video conferencing. Check your answers with a partner and give reasons.

A Quicker decision making

B Lack of personal feeling

C Network / Connection problems

D More collaboration between departments / branches

E Extra setup cost and time

F Cutting out transport (time and money)

G Uninvited guests / Hackers

H Greater efficiency in international business

Advantages	Disadvantages

Scene 1 — ONLINE MEETING

1. LANGUAGE NOTES

WORD BANK — Match the following words with their meanings.

1. layout
2. finding
3. mute
4. region
5. various

a. to turn off a microphone or the audio
b. an area, especially part of a country
c. different kinds
d. the way in which the parts of something are arranged
e. information discovered as the result of a study

PHRASES — Fill in the blanks with the most appropriate phrase from the box. Change the word form wherever necessary.

| get the hang of | suitable for | carry ~ out | get this show on the road | I'm in |

1. I haven't used this machine before, so I need some time to _____ it.
2. A: I don't see Mary yet. Is she joining us later?   B: Hello, _____ now.
3. We have developed a good plan. Now we just need to _____ it _____.
4. I think we've prepared as much as we can. It's time to _____.
5. Pete's new job was _____ him because it met all his requirements.

2. VIDEO WATCHING — CHECK YOUR UNDERSTANDING

FIRST VIEWING — Watch the video of an online conference, and choose the correct answers.

1. What is the reason for having the meeting?
   A. To welcome some new team members
   B. To learn how to use new software
   C. To look at the results of some research
   D. To test new microphones and cameras

2. What will most likely happen next?
   A. They will view some charts.
   B. They will travel to meet each other.
   C. They will finish the meeting.
   D. They will all turn on their microphones.

3. What do people need to do when they are not speaking but listening to others at the online meeting?
   A. Be friendly and smile
   B. Have their microphones turned off
   C. Make a video of other speakers
   D. Show some charts on the screen

UNIT 6 *Video Conferencing*

SECOND VIEWING
Watch the video again and fill in the blanks with the words below.

  1-22

| charts on your screen | video and sound | the number of people |
| the product will be available | the microphone is muted | |

A team of sales representatives has joined an online meeting through the use of video conferencing software.

David: You can choose the layout which you think is most suitable for ① _____ we have.

Oliver: OK. So it looks like everyone has ② _____ except Tim. Oh, wait. Tim, is that you?

Tim: Yes, I'm in! I think I've finally got the hang of this.

David: OK, yes, you need to make sure your camera and microphone are turned on when speaking, and when you're not, make sure ③ _____.

Tim: Got it.

David: The purpose of this meeting is to discuss the findings of a study that was recently carried out by the Marketing Department.

Gemma: We can see several ④ _____.

David: Correct. They represent the interest among various groups for the regions where ⑤ _____.

Tim: I see.

David: I'll take you through each chart, and then everyone will be given some time to comment.

Gemma: Sounds good. Let's get this show on the road.

3. USEFUL EXPRESSIONS

SHADOWING
Listen to the audio and practice saying the sentences below. 1-23

It looks like everyone	has video and sound. is here now.
You need to make sure	the camera is turned on. your microphone is working.
The graphic represents	the interest among various groups. the sales numbers for last year.
I'll take you through	each chart. everything step-by-step.

Scene 2 — PROBLEM SOLVING

1. LANGUAGE NOTES

WORD BANK Fill in the blanks with the most appropriate word from the box. Change the word form wherever necessary.

demonstrate	lag	choppy	barely	temporary

1. The _____ in the audio caused us to talk over each other during the meeting.
2. Julie's job as a waitress is only _____ till she graduates from university.
3. Bill is going to _____ how to use the new machine at the factory.
4. The meeting had to be stopped because the audio was too _____.
5. Stephen _____ remembered using this software before.

PHRASES Fill in the blanks with the most appropriate phrase from the box. Change the word form wherever necessary.

cut out	hard to follow	down to	log out	in sudden bursts

1. Tim _____ of the chat room when he had to leave the meeting early.
2. The speaker was _____ because he spoke with a strong accent.
3. The sound came back _____ during the online meeting.
4. Jane's constant lateness was _____ bad time management.
5. The screen _____ when I accidentally pulled the cable out.

2. VIDEO WATCHING — CHECK YOUR UNDERSTANDING

FIRST VIEWING Watch the video of David in a video conference with three colleagues, and choose the correct answers.

1. What is David trying to show the team?
   - A. Some bar graphs
   - B. Some pie charts
   - C. His camera
   - D. A new computer

2. Why are the team members having problems hearing David?
   - A. He is speaking too quietly.
   - B. His microphone is not working properly.
   - C. They're using a different version of the software.
   - D. The weather is affecting the connection.

3. What will they do if the problem continues?
   - A. Meet face-to-face
   - B. Restart their computers
   - C. Reschedule the meeting
   - D. Cancel the meeting

52

UNIT 6 *Video Conferencing*

SECOND VIEWING   Watch the video again and fill in the blanks.

  1-24

David is showing team members some pie charts which demonstrate market research information.

David: And as you can see in pie chart number three…

Oliver: Sorry, which pie chart is that? Bad connection here.

Gemma: Yeah, I think there's a bit of ①_____, David.

David: I said pie chart three! Can everyone hear me now?

Gemma: Yes, I heard that.

David: Hopefully that was just ②_____. So as I was saying, pie chart three illustrates that consumer interest in the Asia-Pacific region is high for this type of game.

Tim: Oh, ③_____ now, David. Is anyone else having the same problem as me?

David: Hello? Can anyone hear me?

Gemma: Barely, David.

Oliver: Yeah. The picture quality is bad. Also, your sound ④_____ then coming back in sudden bursts. You're very hard to follow.

David: OK, it could be down to bad weather. Let's try logging out of the software and logging back in. If it still doesn't work, we'll have to ⑤_____ until tomorrow.

3. USEFUL EXPRESSIONS

MATCHING   Match the responses with the questions/statements.

Question/Statement	Response
1. We keep talking over each other.	a. Barely.
2. Can you hear me?	b. Let's try logging out and back in again.
3. Why is the connection so bad?	c. It could be down to the bad weather.
4. What should we do?	d. There seems to be a lag in the sound.

Language Practice

Work with a partner and practice the sample phone conversation between staff member A and staff member B. Then create your own conversation, changing the underlined expressions.

A:	I've scheduled an online meeting <u>for tomorrow at 10 a.m.</u>, and I'd like you to join.
B:	OK. How do I gain access to the meeting?
A:	I've sent <u>the link</u> to your e-mail. The meeting room ID is 981 5558 and <u>the password</u> is elite043.
B:	Thanks. What are we going to discuss?
A:	We're going to discuss <u>market research data</u> for the new project <u>that'll be rolled out next month</u>.
B:	Okay. I'll <u>join the meeting right before 10 a.m.</u>
A:	See you at the meeting.

Language Function — Giving instructions

Make sure + you + V

- **Make sure you** turn off the lights after you finish using the room.
- **Make sure you** turn on your camera while you attend the online meeting.

Write your own instructions in the following situations, using "make sure you～," and explain the reasons.

1. (get your ID cards today)

   _____

2. (write up the meeting report by Tuesday)

   _____

3. (have all the materials ready for the meeting tomorrow)

   _____

4. (mute the microphone while listening to others online)

   _____

UNIT 6 *Video Conferencing*

Reading Comprehension

Read the following passage and choose the correct answer.

In recent years, video conferencing systems such as Zoom have become an essential part of business life, especially in large companies. International firms have offices and employees all over the world, so holding face-to-face meetings can require a lot of time and money. Of course, international business can also be done by telephone, but a phone call misses out on a key part of communication: body language.

Some studies have found that body language, especially facial expressions, accounts for up to 80 percent of the meaning we communicate when interacting with other people. Video conferencing solves this problem, and has many other advantages. On the other hand, it also has several downsides.

Firstly, the quality of the meeting depends on the internet connection. If this is bad, meetings can become impossible. Secondly, there is the problem of time zone differences, which make online meetings harder to schedule. Finally, in cultures that rely strongly on personal relationships, video conferencing can seem a cold and impersonal way to interact with colleagues. With face-to-face meetings, people get the chance to make small talk before and after talking business, but this is much harder online. Nevertheless, the time and money it saves companies means that video conferencing is here to stay.

1. How many types of business meetings are mentioned?
    A. One   B. Two   C. Three   D. Four

2. What advantage of video conferencing over phone calls is mentioned?
    A. It is cheaper.
    B. More people can participate.
    C. Participants can see each other's body language.
    D. You can share documents and other information more easily.

3. Which disadvantage of video conferencing is not mentioned?
    A. Technical problems sometimes affect meetings.
    B. Some staff find video conferencing systems too confusing.
    C. Finding a time that suits people in different countries can be difficult.
    D. Video conferencing doesn't help coworkers to build good relationships.

Active Learning

Task 1

You are a product manager hosting an online video conference. Write an email to your staff and give information on the schedule, the URL link, and the agenda, using the form below.

To:

From:

Subject:

Dear colleagues,

Date:	Time:
Host:	Meeting Room ID:
Link URL:	
Password:	

Thank you,

Product Manager

Task 2

Your company is helping small cafés and restaurants promote their business using social media. Research some cafés and restaurants that are efficiently using social media and analyze their features. Make a list of good ways of using social media and present it to the owners of the cafés and restaurants either face-to-face or online. Work in a pair or a group of three or four.

UNIT 7 Review 1

A ▶ VOCABULARY I — Matching

Match the following words with their meanings. (There are two extra definitions.)

1. security •
2. employee •
3. available •
4. appear •
5. branch •
6. various •

- a. to seem, to look like
- b. different kinds
- c. to prepare for
- d. safety
- e. free, not busy
- f. an area, especially part of a country
- g. someone who is paid to work for someone else
- h. smaller office or store, local office or store

B ▶ VOCABULARY II — Gap Filling

Fill in the blanks with the most appropriate word from the box.
Change the word form wherever necessary. (There are two extra words.)

1. A: Sorry for the wait.   B: It's no _____ at all.
2. Tyron _____ the schedule to me at the last meeting.
3. It says on your _____ that you have previous experience with two companies.
4. I need someone to cover my _____ next Friday because I have a wedding to attend.
5. Always _____ your guests their meals first at the dinner table.
6. Bill is going to _____ how to use the new machine at the factory.

| explain | purpose | serve | bother |
| application | demonstrate | postpone | shift |

C ▶ PHRASES — Gap Filling

Fill in the blanks with the most appropriate phrase from the box.
Change the word form wherever necessary. (There is one extra expression.)

1. _____ the General Manager of Unicorp, I welcome all of you.
2. A: Thank you for your advice.   B: _____.
3. Please _____ more drinks if you like.
4. Paige forgot to _____ yesterday morning.
5. Hannah will _____ me _____ later this afternoon.
6. I'm busy right now. Do you mind if I _____ you after lunch?
7. This is a busy time of year, so you can't _____ next week.
8. Employees are demanding the company give them _____.

call ~ back	on behalf of	take time off
overtime pay	help yourself to	get back to
clock in	make sure	my pleasure

57

D PHOTOGRAPHS

Listen and choose the sentence that best describes the photo.

1.
   A.   B.   C.   D.

2.
   A.   B.   C.   D.

3.
   A.   B.   C.   D.

4.
   A.   B.   C.   D.

E QUESTION AND RESPONSE

Listen and choose the best response to the sentence you hear.

1.	A	B	C	6.	A	B	C
2.	A	B	C	7.	A	B	C
3.	A	B	C	8.	A	B	C
4.	A	B	C	9.	A	B	C
5.	A	B	C	10.	A	B	C

F ▶ SHORT CONVERSATION

 1-40, 41

Listen to a short conversation and answer the questions.

1. What is happening?
    - A. A meeting is being arranged.
    - B. A meeting is about to start.
    - C. A presentation is in progress.
    - D. A presentation is about to finish.

2. What does Harry do to help Jake hear him more clearly?
    - A. Change the microphone
    - B. Turn his volume up
    - C. Move nearer the microphone
    - D. Restart the software

3. Why was Jill's screen choppy?
    - A. She was using an old computer.
    - B. She was using the wrong setting.
    - C. She had a bad internet connection.
    - D. She had too many apps open.

G ▶ SHORT TALK

 1-42, 43

Listen to a short talk and answer the questions.

1. What is the purpose of the call?
    - A. To complain about something
    - B. To follow up on a recent meeting
    - C. To cancel an appointment
    - D. To change an appointment time

2. What contact information does she give for herself?
    - A. A telephone number
    - B. A fax number
    - C. A company address
    - D. An e-mail address

3. Why can't Ms. Reeves meet Mr. Jenkins this afternoon?
    - A. She has another important appointment.
    - B. She has to deal with something urgently.
    - C. She doesn't want to work with him.
    - D. She forgot about the appointment.

H ▶ INCOMPLETE SENTENCES

Choose the best word to complete each sentence.

1. Allen works very hard to _____ the goals that he sets for himself.
   - A. invite
   - B. accomplish
   - C. report
   - D. contact

2. We must _____ the conference room for next week's meeting.
   - A. reserve
   - B. announce
   - C. lead
   - D. end

3. When you visit someone, they will usually offer you some sort of _____.
   - A. attention
   - B. refreshments
   - C. branches
   - D. invitations

4. Please take time to review your report before you _____ it.
   - A. arrange
   - B. receive
   - C. submit
   - D. serve

5. Our manager hasn't _____ this suggestion yet, so we can't continue.
   - A. appeared
   - B. presented
   - C. rented
   - D. approved

6. The project's excellent results _____ lots of planning and hard work.
   - A. rolled out
   - B. were down to
   - C. gained access to
   - D. carried out

7. You should turn the volume up because I can _____ hear what you're saying.
   - A. suitably
   - B. clearly
   - C. barely
   - D. only

8. The scientist did a talk at our college about her latest _____.
   - A. regions
   - B. bursts
   - C. layouts
   - D. findings

9. I called this meeting today because there are some company changes that you all need to be _____ of.
   - A. aware
   - B. brand-new
   - C. various
   - D. temporary

10. In order to get into the meeting room, the _____ needs to send you a link.
    - A. data
    - B. host
    - C. connection
    - D. lag

60

UNIT 7 Review 1

I ▶ TEXT COMPLETION

Select the best answer to complete the text.

To all employees:

The company is making changes to its ①_____. Please look at the list below

        A. supplies   **B.** policies

        C. teams   **D.** training

to see more information about these changes.

1.   From now on, your ②_____ will be only 45 minutes. There are

        A. lunch break   **B.** coffee maker

        C. break room   **D.** water cooler

many restaurants near the office, ③_____.

        A. and you must wear your ID badge

        B. but they're quite far away

        C. so you can take more time

        D. so this shouldn't be a problem

2.   Everyone must wear their ④_____ badge when they are in the office.

        A. coworker   **B.** notepad

        C. supply   **D.** ID

3.   The ⑤_____ will no longer be used for clocking in and out. You must do

        A. corner   **B.** scanner

        C. copier   **D.** account

it on your computer.

If you have any questions, please see your manager.

Sincerely,

Management

UNIT 7

61

J READING

Read the following passage and answer the questions.

Generally, the larger the size of a company, the more likely it is to require video conferencing. International firms have offices and employees all over the world, and flying a team of people into the same location requires time and money. In the past, businesses could make phone calls, but a phone call misses out on a key part of communication: body language. Studies have found that body language, especially in the form of facial expressions, indicates up to 80% of the meaning we communicate when interacting. While video conferencing solves this problem, it has various downsides. Firstly, the quality of the meeting depends entirely on your internet connection so, if this is bad, your meeting will be affected. Secondly, there are potentially high setup costs as well as staff training. Thirdly, there is the issue of time zone differences, which make online meetings harder to schedule. Nevertheless, all of these obstacles have solutions, and video conferencing is sure to continue its rise in the coming years.

1. What is the main purpose of the article?
   A. To suggest that small businesses buy video conferencing software
   B. To report the advantages and disadvantages of video conferencing
   C. To make predictions about the future of business meetings
   D. To argue for the importance of body language in communication

2. According to the article, what is most important when communicating meaning?
   A. Vocabulary   B. Tone of voice
   C. Facial expressions   D. Hand signals

3. Which of the following is most similar in meaning to the word "obstacles" in the reading?
   A. Challenges   B. Capacities
   C. Considerations   D. Corporations

UNIT 8

Job Interviews

✓ Checklist

In this unit, you will learn about...
- Answering questions and promoting yourself in a job interview
- Asking about the job and the company

Warm-up

Give yourself a score for each quality, with 0 being the worst and 5 being the best. Share your graphic with your classmates and discuss which quality is the most important at work.

Other: _____

63

Scene 1 — TALKING ABOUT YOURSELF

1. LANGUAGE NOTES

WORD BANK — Match the following words with their meanings.

1. personnel
2. résumé
3. proficient
4. interviewee
5. exaggerate

a. skillful, capable
b. a person who answers questions when looking for a job
c. to make something seem better than it really is
d. staff, human resources, workforce
e. CV, a short summary of work experience

PHRASES — Fill in the blanks with the most appropriate phrase from the box. Change the word form wherever necessary.

| know something about | tech industry | picture yourself | tend to | prefer to |

1. I _____ be honest about my work skills at interviews.
2. Where do you _____ in 10 years?
3. I worked for a fashion brand, so I _____ the textile industry.
4. People _____ be nervous before job interviews.
5. John has been working in the _____ for the last 20 years.

2. VIDEO WATCHING — CHECK YOUR UNDERSTANDING

FIRST VIEWING — Watch the video of Mrs. Becker, the personnel manager, interviewing Sam, and choose the correct answers.

1. Which of the following skills or qualifications does Sam not have?
   A. Word processing
   B. Making spreadsheets
   C. Setting up databases
   D. Selling over the phone

2. Which part of Sam's personality does Mrs. Becker think is impressive?
   A. His organizational skills
   B. His honesty
   C. His ability to work in a team
   D. His desire to work hard

3. What kind of job is Sam most probably applying for?
   A. Computer technician
   B. Data entry clerk
   C. Sales representative
   D. Web designer

64

UNIT 8 *Job Interviews*

SECOND VIEWING
Watch the video again and fill in the blanks with the words below.

 1-44

| I like your honesty | in a senior sales position | ability to learn fast |
| proficient in word processing | work well with others | |

Mrs. Becker, the personnel manager, is interviewing Sam.

Mrs. Becker: So your résumé says you've worked at several companies.

Sam: Yes, and in my last job, I worked for DigiSky, so I know something about the tech industry.

Mrs. Becker: That's good. How are your computer skills?

Sam: I'm ①_____, creating spreadsheets and setting up databases. I also have experience making web pages.

Mrs. Becker: Impressive. How would you describe yourself?

Sam: I'm hardworking, organized, and ②_____.

Mrs. Becker: Where do you picture yourself in five years?

Sam: I want to be ③_____ with a tech company.

Mrs. Becker: And do you have any experience in sales?

Sam: Actually, I don't. But I believe my personality and ④_____ will make me a good sales rep.

Mrs. Becker: ⑤_____. Some interviewees tend to exaggerate.

Sam: I prefer to be honest. No one likes to be cheated, including potential customers.

3. USEFUL EXPRESSIONS

MATCHING
Match the responses with the questions/statements.

Question/Statement	Response
1. Could you please briefly describe yourself?	a. Yes, I have more than ten years of experience.
2. Do you have experience in the auto industry?	b. I'm familiar with word processing, spreadsheets, and presentation applications.
3. Tell me about your computer skills.	c. I'm very responsible and always have a smile on my face.
4. Are you willing to work overtime?	d. I can work late from time to time.

65

Scene 2 ▶ ASKING ABOUT THE JOB

1. LANGUAGE NOTES

WORD BANK **Fill in the blanks with the most appropriate word from the box. Change the word form wherever necessary.**

explain	brochure	supervisor	recommend	insurance

1. I got my current position because Mr. Smith _____ me for it.

2. Let me _____ about the company's new policy.

3. This _____ shows the products we offer.

4. Do you have _____ on your car?

5. Can you tell us who the project _____ would be?

PHRASES **Fill in the blanks with the most appropriate phrase from the box. Change the word form wherever necessary.**

compensation package	entry-level	follow-up	paid vacation	feel free to

1. The _____ salary will be $30,000 a year.

2. I'll introduce you to our _____, which includes full health insurance.

3. Do you have any _____ questions?

4. All the workers have two weeks' _____ a year.

5. _____ look around the office and talk to people.

2. VIDEO WATCHING   CHECK YOUR UNDERSTANDING

FIRST VIEWING **Watch the video of Sam asking Mrs. Becker about the job and the company, and choose the correct answers.**

WEB動画

1. Which area of business is Mrs. Becker's company currently trying to develop?

   A. Insurance plans   B. Public relations

   C. Company brochures   D. Online sales

2. How much paid holiday would Sam receive annually if he was hired?

   A. Two days   B. Twelve days   C. Fourteen days   D. Twenty days

3. What is the result of the interview?

   A. Sam is recommended for another position.

   B. Sam will return for a second interview.

   C. Sam is offered a position in the company.

   D. Sam is not offered a position in the company.

66

UNIT 8 *Job Interviews*

SECOND VIEWING   Watch the video again and fill in the blanks.

Sam is asking Mrs. Becker about the job and the company.

Sam: Could you tell me about the company's future plans?

Mrs. Becker: Yes, our big focus now is on ①_____. It's all explained in our company brochure. Here.

Sam: Thank you. And who would be my supervisor?

Mrs. Becker: You'd report to ②_____.

Sam: I see. Does the job require much travel?

Mrs. Becker: Yes, our salespeople are on the road a lot ③_____. Any more questions?

Sam: I can't think of any others at this time.

Mrs. Becker: Well, let me introduce ④_____ to you. We offer our entry-level salespeople an annual salary of $30,000, plus full health insurance and two weeks' paid vacation.

Sam: That sounds good.

Mrs. Becker: I've certainly enjoyed meeting with you, Sam. You seem like a strong candidate for this position. I'll recommend you for ⑤_____ with the sales manager.

Sam: Thank you very much.

Mrs. Becker: Good luck. Feel free to call me if you have any questions.

3. USEFUL EXPRESSIONS

SHADOWING   Listen to the audio and practice saying the sentences below.

Asking about the job

1. Does the job require much travel or overtime?
2. Are we required to wear a uniform?
3. Is it necessary for us to clock in?
4. Do you provide health insurance?
5. Does the company have parking?
6. Could you tell me about the benefits you offer?
7. Would you please fill me in on what my role will be?

Language Practice

Work with a partner and practice the sample phone conversation between a manager and an interviewee. Then create your own conversation, changing the underlined expressions.

Manager:	May I ask what attracted you to our <u>service manager</u> position, <u>Mrs. Whitson</u>?
Interviewee:	Certainly. I have a lot of experience <u>in hospitality</u>, and becoming a manager is the next step for me.
Manager:	Do you have a minimum of two years' experience in the industry?
Interviewee:	I have <u>five years</u> of experience <u>as a front desk clerk at Carlton</u>. That job exposed me to a wide range of issues and I constantly had to solve problems.
Manager:	Sounds impressive. Do you have a <u>hospitality-related</u> degree?
Interviewee:	Yes. I earned a BA in <u>hotel management</u> from <u>Whiteside University</u>.
Manager:	Well, I think <u>you're a good candidate</u>. I'll recommend you for another interview.

Examples of industries

• art	• finance	• manufacturing	• restaurant
• auto	• fashion	• medical	• space
• construction	• food	• movie	• sports
• design	• hotel	• music	• tech
• education	• insurance	• publishing	• textile

Language Function ▶ Talking about one's experience

have experience + V ～ing (gerund)

- **_I have experience_** mak**ing** web pages.   - **_I have_** 3 years of **_experience_** arrang**ing** conferences

Write about your own experience in the following areas and add a further comment.

1. (create marketing campaigns for a global sports brand)

   _____

2. (do research on hybrid cars in Japan and Germany, 10 years)

   _____

3. (make wooden toys, 5 years)

   _____

UNIT 8 *Job Interviews*

Reading Comprehension

Read the following passage and choose **T** if the statement is true, or **F** if it is false. 1-47

Success in job interviews depends on many things, but none is more important than the interviewer's first impression. One study found that one third of interviewers decided whether or not to hire someone within the first 90 seconds of the interview.

Fortunately, there are many things you can do to make sure you give a positive first impression. Of course, you should dress smartly, and leave plenty of time for your journey to avoid feeling rushed or stressed. At the start of the interview, smile, and be sure to sound confident. Look the interviewer in the eye and make it clear that you are listening carefully. Before the interview, it is a good idea to research the company, and make sure you are familiar with industry trends. That way, you can give detailed answers with specific examples.

Most importantly, it is best to be honest. If the interviewer asks about your weaknesses, answer truthfully but remember to also explain what you have done to overcome them. After all, finding solutions to challenges is an important skill. At the end of the interview, don't forget to thank the interviewer for their time. Giving a good final impression is also very important!

1. Half of all hiring decisions are made in less than two minutes. T☐ F☐
2. Both body language and your tone of voice are important to making a good first impression. T☐ F☐
3. You should avoid looking the interviewer straight in the eye as it is considered rude. T☐ F☐
4. Careful preparation before the interview can help you answer questions with examples. T☐ F☐
5. You should not explain your weaknesses since this gives you a disadvantage in the interview. T☐ F☐

Active Learning

Task 1

In a Word document, create your own one-page résumé / CV (Curriculum Vitae) with personal details, education, and qualifications, as well as work experience.

Notes: An English CV does not have a specific format like a Japanese CV. You can create your own format. Here is a sample format below. You can list your part-time work if you don't have full-time work experience. List your education and work experience in chronological order (list the latest experience at the top.)

Curriculum Vitae

▶ **Personal Details** ....

▶ **Work Experience** ....

▶ **Education** ....

▶ **Qualifications** ....

Task 2

You are at a job interview. Please explain about your CV and answer the questions the interviewers ask. Tell the interviewers your strengths and explain why you are qualified for the job. As interviewers, ask the interviewee some questions based on the CV he or she submitted. Work in a pair or a group of three or four and switch roles.

UNIT 9
Traveling on Business

Checklist

In this unit, you will learn about...
- Arriving at the airport
- Checking into a hotel

Warm-up

Number the steps you take (1 = first, 6 = last) in preparing for business trips.
Check the answers with a partner. Add comments/tips on each stage of preparation.

- [ ] Prepare a well-thought-out itinerary
- [ ] Bring business cards
- [ ] Book your accommodations early
- [ ] Set up internet
- [ ] Read your company's travel policy
- [ ] Take carry-on luggage only

Scene 1 — BEING PICKED UP

1. LANGUAGE NOTES

WORD BANK — Match the following words with their meanings.

1. arrival
2. delay
3. pleasant
4. in-flight
5. grab

a. being late or slow
b. coming, appearance, entrance
c. during the plane journey
d. nice, comfortable
e. to get

PHRASES — Fill in the blanks with the most appropriate phrase from the box. Change the word form wherever necessary.

| hold up | in no time | in that case | head out | I'm good |

1. The traffic is very light today, so we'll be in the city _____.
2. What time are you _____ tomorrow?
3. A: Do you want anything from the store?   B: No, _____. Thanks for asking.
4. James noticed a man _____ a sign with his name on it.
5. You're going to be late? _____, I'll go and sit in a local café for a while.

2. VIDEO WATCHING — CHECK YOUR UNDERSTANDING

FIRST VIEWING — Watch the video of Mr. Scott being met at the arrivals gate in Chicago, and choose the correct answers.

1. What did Mr. Scott hear about during his flight?
    A. He heard traffic news affecting the bus service from the airport.
    B. He heard that the arrival time was going to be delayed.
    C. He heard that the weather at the destination was good.
    D. He heard about recommended local restaurants in the city.

2. What will Mr. Scott do after relaxing by the pool later?
    A. Go to a meeting
    B. Watch TV
    C. Eat something
    D. Check the weather

3. What will Rupert and Mr. Scott do next?
    A. Grab something to eat
    B. Get on the plane
    C. Go to the baggage claim
    D. Go to the car

72

UNIT 9 *Traveling on Business*

SECOND VIEWING
Watch the video again and fill in the blanks with the words below.

| No delays | Please allow me | grab anything to eat |
| looking forward to relaxing | head out to the car | |

Mr. Scott has just landed in Chicago and is walking through the arrivals gate. He notices a man holding up a sign with his name on it.

Rupert: Hello, Mr. Scott from Viox International?

Mr. Scott: Yes, that's me.

Rupert: I am Rupert, your driver. ① _____ to take your bag. Did you have a pleasant flight, sir?

Mr. Scott: Thanks, Rupert. Yes, it was fine. ② _____, and according to the in-flight information, it's a beautiful sunny day out there.

Rupert: Yes, that's correct. The weather has been lovely recently. And the streets are pretty quiet now, so we'll be in the city in no time.

Mr. Scott: That's good to know. I'm ③ _____ by the hotel pool for a few hours before the meeting tonight.

Rupert: Sounds wonderful. Oh, by the way, would you like to ④ _____ before we get going?

Mr. Scott: No need. I had something on the plane so I'm good for now.

Rupert: OK. In that case, let's ⑤ _____. Right this way, Mr. Scott.

3. USEFUL EXPRESSIONS

SHADOWING
Listen to the audio and practice saying the sentences below.

1. **Traveler:** How long will it take to get to the hotel?
   Host: It'll take about 45 minutes.

2. **Host:** Would you like to grab anything to eat?
   Traveler: I'm good for now.
   Host: In that case, let's head out to the car.

3. **Traveler:** Could I exchange some currency before we get going?
   Host: Sure. The money exchange counter is right around the corner.

73

Scene 2 — ACCOMMODATIONS

1. LANGUAGE NOTES

WORD BANK — Fill in the blanks with the most appropriate word from the box. Change the word form wherever necessary.

unzip	compartment	remove	details	transportation

1. Taking public _____ to the airport is easier than driving.
2. He reached into his bag and _____ the paperwork from the folder.
3. This booklet gives you some _____ about the hotel.
4. The security guard asked Jim to _____ his bag and take the computer out.
5. After we boarded the plane, we put our carry-on bags in the overhead _____.

PHRASES — Fill in the blanks with the most appropriate phrase from the box. Change the word form wherever necessary.

drop ~ off	get ~ sorted	check in	on business	just a second

1. Bill asked the taxi driver to _____ him _____ on the street corner.
2. A: Are you ready to go?   B: _____. I'll get my hat.
3. I've _____ the visa _____, so now I just need to book the flight.
4. I'm here _____ for three days.
5. I arrived a little earlier, but can I _____ now?

2. VIDEO WATCHING — CHECK YOUR UNDERSTANDING

FIRST VIEWING — Watch the video of Mr. Scott checking in at his hotel, and choose the correct answers.

1. Where can Mr. Scott find Wi-Fi information?
   - A. On his keycard
   - B. In the business center
   - C. In his room
   - D. On a sign

2. What kind of room does Mr. Scott ask for?
   - A. A room with a wonderful view
   - B. A room with internet access
   - C. A room that isn't noisy
   - D. A room on the sixth floor

3. Where is the business center?
   - A. At the end of the hallway
   - B. To the left of the hallway
   - C. Down the sixth floor hallway
   - D. In room 142 on the ninth floor

UNIT 9 *Traveling on Business*

SECOND VIEWING   Watch the video again and fill in the blanks.

Mr. Scott has just been dropped off at his hotel and is about to check in.

Mr. Scott: Hi, I'm here to check in.

Hotel Clerk: Welcome to the Sunshine Hotel. Could I have your passport and check-in information, please?

Mr. Scott: Yes, just a second. *(He removes the requested documents from his travel case.)*
① _____ .

Hotel Clerk: Thank you.

Mr. Scott: Can I get the Wi-Fi log-in information, please?

Hotel Clerk: Yes, the Wi-Fi ② _____ on the sign here. *(Points to a sign.)*

Mr. Scott: I'm here on business, so I'd like a quiet room if possible.

Hotel Clerk: No problem. You're in room ③ _____ . It faces a quiet street.

Mr. Scott: Perfect. What time is the business center open until?

Hotel Clerk: It's ④ _____ and it's on this floor, down the hallway to my left here. Last door on the right. Will you be needing ⑤ _____ on Sunday, Mr. Scott?

Mr. Scott: That won't be necessary. I've got a pickup sorted. Thanks for your help.

Hotel Clerk: My pleasure. Have a wonderful stay.

3. USEFUL EXPRESSIONS

MAKING QUESTIONS   Create a question for the answers given. Then, practice using them with a partner.

1. **Q** Could I _____?
   A Yes, just a second *(Pause)*. Here you are.

2. **Q** Can I _____?
   A Yes, the network name and password are written on the sign here.

3. **Q** Is there _____?
   A Sure. I'll put you in room 80 on the 12th floor. There are no other rooms on either side.

4. **Q** What time _____?
   A It closes at 10 p.m.

Language Practice

Work with a partner and practice the sample phone conversation between a member of staff at a company and a client from overseas. Then create your own conversation, changing the underlined expressions.

Client:	Hi Stephen. This is <u>Jane from The Hill Group</u>. I've got details of Mr. Hill's trip for you here.
Staff:	<u>Nice to hear from you, Jane</u>. Great. Can I get the flight number, arrival date, and time, please?
Client:	The flight number is <u>BE642</u>. That's <u>B for bravo</u>. <u>Mr. Hill's flight</u> touches down at <u>9:15 a.m.</u> local time on <u>the morning of the 5th of March</u>.
Staff:	All right. Thank you for the flight information. Where is he staying?
Client:	He's staying at <u>The Milton Hotel in the city center</u>.
Staff:	<u>That's a nice hotel</u>. Will <u>Mr. Hill</u> be needing an airport pickup?
Client:	Yes. Please arrange someone <u>to take him to his hotel</u>. Thank you.
Staff:	<u>Okay, we'll do that</u>.

Language Function — Telling someone things have been taken care of

have got + N + V + ed

- I've **got** my desk **organized**. I'm ready to work.
- I've **got** a hotel **booked**. It's a nice hotel near the beach.

Write sentences explaining that the following things are taken care of and add a further comment.

1. (a visa / sort / my first trip to Brazil)

   _____

2. (that office problem / solve / relax this weekend)

   _____

3. (an airport pickup / arrange / the driver / meet me / the airport)

   _____

4. (a rental car / organize / drive to the hotel)

   _____

76

Reading Comprehension

Read the following passage and choose the correct answer.

 1-51

For many years, a common feature of large international hotels has been a business center — a space in which facilities such as computers, fax machines, and photocopiers are provided. For people traveling on business, access to these facilities was essential for their trip. These days, however, hotel business centers are becoming less and less necessary, as almost all business people will travel with their own laptop computer, and will rarely need to send a fax or copy a physical document.

For most people, the only business-related facility that a hotel now needs to provide is a strong and reliable Wi-Fi connection. Technology has been changing the way business travelers experience hotels in other ways, too. Many hotels now use robots to carry out jobs previously done by humans. You may encounter a robot cleaning an elevator, delivering your room service order to your room, or even greeting you at the front desk when you arrive.

While some of these robots look and act like simple machines, others resemble humans and make use of AI to interact with guests, often in several different languages. These robots are usually highly efficient and can help your stay go smoothly. Even so, for situations involving problems or complaints, most guests would probably still prefer the assistance of a human employee.

1. Which is the most important service that hotels should offer business travelers these days?
    A. Good Wi-Fi
    B. Robot assistants
    C. A well-equipped business center
    D. Laptop computers that they can rent

2. Which job is better suited to people than to robots?
    A. Serving food
    B. Talking to guests
    C. Changing bed linen
    D. Dealing with customer service issues

3. What is the main point of this passage?
    A. AI is gradually taking over humans' jobs.
    B. Traveling on business is becoming easier.
    C. Technology has changed various aspects of hotels.
    D. Hotels need to invest a lot of money in new equipment.

Active Learning

Task 1

You and your colleague are going on a business trip abroad. Choose a country or city and prepare an itinerary with business meetings on one day and sightseeing activities on the other. Share your plan with your colleague and get some feedback.

Business Meetings	Off-Day Activities
Date:	Morning (Places to visit):
Time:	
Place (City):	
Agenda:	Afternoon (Places to visit):
Participants:	Night Activities:

Task 2

You and your colleague are looking for a hotel for a business trip. Decide which country you are visiting, then look into two hotels and compare their prices and features. Discuss them with your colleague and decide on the hotel you will be staying at.

1	2
Location:	Location:
Name:	Name:
Price:	Price:
Size:	Size:
View:	View:
Facilities:	Facilities:
Others:	Others:

UNIT 10
Receiving Overseas Visitors

Checklist

In this unit, you will learn about...
- Picking up a visitor
- Showing a visitor around your workplace

Warm-up

Fill in the blanks with the most appropriate word from the box to complete the tips. Decide which tips you would be most likely to follow. Then, check the answers with a partner. (There is one extra word in the box.)

| brief | directions | entrance | greet | refreshments |

HOW TO MAKE OVERSEAS VISITORS FEEL WELCOME IN YOUR OFFICE

✓ _____ your staff on the guest's visit.

✓ Assign someone to _____ and welcome your client.

✓ Give clear _____.

✓ Address the client by his/her first name.

✓ Offer _____.

Scene 1 — AT THE AIRPORT

1. LANGUAGE NOTES

WORD BANK Match the following words with their definitions.

1. publisher
2. luggage
3. client
4. normal
5. surprising

a. usual, typical, common
b. shocking, amazing
c. a company that produces books or songs
d. customer, buyer, user
e. bags, baggage

PHRASES Fill in the blanks with the most appropriate phrase from the box. Change the word form wherever necessary.

| pick up | give ~ a hand | put ~ away | for a bit | get to |

1. You've been working hard all week. You should relax _____.
2. Please _____ everything _____ and clear the table.
3. Can you _____ me _____? This is very heavy.
4. John is going to _____ our guests from Spain at the airport today.
5. Did you _____ meet Lizzie while she was here?

2. VIDEO WATCHING — CHECK YOUR UNDERSTANDING

FIRST VIEWING Watch the video of Joseph picking up a client from Canada. Answer T (true) or F (false) based on the conversation.

1. Joseph and Tonya have met before in Canada. T☐ F☐
2. Tonya didn't like the food she had on the plane. T☐ F☐
3. Tonya enjoyed watching some movies on her flight. T☐ F☐
4. Joseph and Tonya must call a taxi to go to the hotel. T☐ F☐

UNIT 10 *Receiving Overseas Visitors*

SECOND VIEWING

Watch the video again and fill in the blanks with the words below.

  1-52

| take us to your hotel | finally meet you | slept most of the time |
| didn't taste very good | giving me a hand | |

Joseph is at the airport to pick up a client from Canada.

Joseph: Excuse me. Are you Tonya from Origin Publishers?

Tonya: Yes. I'm Tonya from Origin Publishers.

Joseph: It's nice to ①_____. I'm Joseph. May I help you with your luggage?

Tonya: Yes, please. Thanks for ②_____, Joseph.

Joseph: It's no problem. So, how was your flight? I hope you had a pleasant trip.

Tonya: It was OK. The food ③_____, but I think that's normal for food served on an airplane.

Joseph: That's true. Did you get to watch any movies?

Tonya: No. I ④_____. Traveling always makes me tired.

Joseph: With such a long trip, that's not surprising. Well, we can go if you're ready. We have a car outside waiting to ⑤_____.

Tonya: Great. I'd like to put all my stuff away and relax for a bit.

3. USEFUL EXPRESSIONS

SHADOWING

Listen to the audio and practice saying the sentences below with a partner.

 1-53

	Receiver	Guest
1.	Excuse me. Are you Sarah Harper of Electronics Unlimited?	I am. I appreciate you picking me up.
2.	Ms. Reynolds? I'm Jason from LCE Industries.	Glad to meet you.
3.	How was your flight? I hope you had a pleasant trip.	There was a bit of turbulence near the end, but it was fine overall.
4.	May I help you with your luggage?	Thanks. If you could take this rolling bag, I can handle the rest.
5.	We have a car waiting outside.	I'll follow you then.

| Scene 2 | A COMPANY TOUR |

1. LANGUAGE NOTES

WORD BANK Fill in the blanks with the most appropriate word from the box. Change the word form wherever necessary.

| secretary | accounting | favorite | CEO | coworker |

1. Marisa Smith works as a _____ to the president.

2. My _____ task at work is talking to new customers.

3. Let me introduce you to our _____, Joi Williams. She started the company 8 years ago.

4. I get on well with all my new _____.

5. I could never work in _____. I'm terrible at math!

PHRASES Fill in the blanks with the most appropriate phrase from the box. Change the word form wherever necessary.

| on the agenda | show ~ around | go over | try out | face-to-face |

1. What's _____ for today's meeting?

2. New staff members are going to have a _____ meeting tomorrow.

3. Linda will _____ you _____ the office when you come.

4. On my first day, my trainer _____ my employment contract with me.

5. We _____ a new system at the office, but it didn't work well.

2. VIDEO WATCHING   CHECK YOUR UNDERSTANDING

FIRST VIEWING Watch the video of Joseph taking Tonya on a tour of his company. Answer **T** (true) or **F** (false) based on the conversation.

WEB動画

1. Megan is a secretary working for the CEO of the company.   T☐   F☐

2. Mr. Jackson is in charge of the sales department.   T☐   F☐

3. Sam is responsible for accounting.   T☐   F☐

4. Megan will go with Tonya to lunch.   T☐   F☐

UNIT 10 *Receiving Overseas Visitors*

SECOND VIEWING   Watch the video again and fill in the blanks.

  1-54

Joseph takes Tonya on a tour of his company.

Joseph: Welcome, Tonya. I hope you had a pleasant evening.

Tonya: I did. Thank you very much. What's ①_____ for today?

Joseph: I'm going to ②_____ and introduce you to some important people here.

Tonya: Great. I'm ③_____ your coworkers.

Joseph: This is Megan. She's Mr. Jackson's secretary, so when you call the CEO's office, you'll talk to her first.

Tonya: I think I've talked to you before. It's nice to meet you face-to-face.

Megan: It's nice to finally meet you, too.

Joseph: And this is Sam. ④_____. He'll go over the details of your company's account with us this afternoon.

Tonya: Pleased to meet you.

Sam: Glad to meet you, too. After we finish our business, I'd like to take you to one of my favorite restaurants for lunch.

Tonya: ⑤_____. I'd love to try out the local food.

3. USEFUL EXPRESSIONS   SAMPLE OF ORGANIZATIONAL CHART

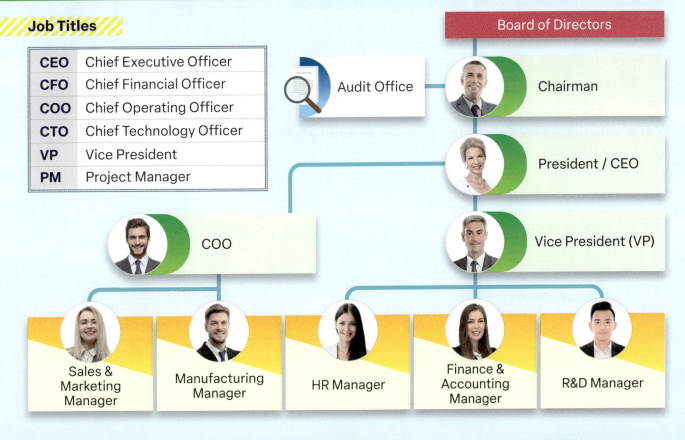

83

Language Practice

Work with a partner and practice the sample phone conversation between a member of staff at a company and a client from overseas. Then create your own conversation, changing the underlined expressions

Staff:	Welcome to our company, <u>Elizabeth</u>. I'm going to <u>take you on a tour of the office</u>.
Guest:	<u>That sounds good</u>. Will I get to meet any of your coworkers?
Staff:	Yes. I'm going to introduce you to Sarah, <u>who is in charge of Sales and Marketing</u>.
Guest:	Great. I look forward to <u>meeting her</u>.
Staff:	Also, if <u>John is in the office</u>, I'll introduce you to him. <u>He's an R&D manager</u>.
Guest:	That's wonderful. I'd like to meet him, <u>if he's available</u>.
Staff:	After I show you around the office, <u>we can have lunch at a restaurant nearby</u>.
Guest:	<u>Sounds like a good plan</u>.

Language Function — Offering to help

help + someone + with N **help + someone + verb**

- Can I help you with your luggage? You must be tired after a long flight.
- Do you need help with the dishes? That'll be quicker.
- Do you want me to help you carry your bag?

Offer your help in the following situations and add a further comment.

1. (project)

   _____

2. (PowerPoint slides)

   _____

3. (move heavy boxes)

   _____

4. (make copies of the documents for the meeting)

   _____

84

UNIT 10 *Receiving Overseas Visitors*

Reading Comprehension

Read the following passage and choose **T** if the statement is true, or **F** if it is false. 1-55

When clients or business associates visit your company from abroad, it is both good manners and good business to make them welcome and help their trip go smoothly. An effective way to do this is to put yourself in their shoes. In other words, think about what you need help with when you are on an overseas business trip.

One example may be getting into the city from the airport. If you don't speak the local language, arriving in a new country can be the most stressful part of the trip. Arranging for a driver to meet your visitors at the airport will get things off to a good start. If your guests come directly to your office, they will probably be tired from the journey, so it is better not to talk business right away.

Misunderstandings might also occur if you are not familiar with each other's customs. However, this is normal, and it is a good chance to learn about different ways of doing things. Sometimes on longer business trips, the visitors may have time for socializing and sightseeing, so in that case think of some nice restaurants or interesting spots you could take them to. And remember that in the future, the roles could be reversed, and you might be the visitor.

1. When clients visit from overseas, being a good host can benefit your company. T☐ F☐
2. Organizing transportation for your guests might cause them more stress. T☐ F☐
3. It is a good idea to begin meetings as soon as your guests arrive. T☐ F☐
4. Cultural differences should not be thought of as a problem. T☐ F☐
5. A host company is required to entertain overseas visitors with leisure activities. T☐ F☐

Active Learning

Task 1

You and your colleague are looking for a restaurant for your foreign clients. Choose two restaurants, compare their features, and make a decision on which is the best option. Work in pairs or groups.

1
Location:
Name:
Price Range:
Specialty:

2
Location:
Name:
Price Range:
Specialty:

Task 2

You and your colleague are going to take some clients from overseas on one-day tours of Tokyo and Kyoto. Make suitable itineraries for your clients and explain the plan to them. Work in pairs or groups.

Tour in Tokyo
Morning (Places to visit)
Afternoon (Places to visit)
Night Activities

Tour in Kyoto
Morning (Places to visit)
Afternoon (Places to visit)
Night Activities

UNIT 11
Meeting with Clients

Checklist

In this unit, you will learn about...
- Introducing a company's history
- Giving information about products and services

Warm-up

Which do you consider to be the most effective ways for a company to reach new clients? Select three options from below and discuss your reasons with a partner.

☐ TV & radio commercials

☐ E-mail marketing

☐ Telemarketing (Telephone marketing)

☐ Direct marketing letters (DM)

☐ Trade shows

☐ Face-to-face selling

☐ Online advertisements

☐ Surveys or polls

☐ Company websites & blogs

Scene 1 — COMPANY INTRODUCTIONS

1. LANGUAGE NOTES

WORD BANK Match the following words with their definitions.

1. found
2. manufacturer
3. worldwide
4. headquarters
5. impressive

a. global / globally
b. main office
c. a person or company that makes goods for sale
d. amazing, remarkable, splendid
e. to establish, to set up

PHRASES Fill in the blanks with the most appropriate phrase from the box. Change the word form wherever necessary.

| familiar with | start out as | a wide range of | based in | have no idea |

1. Most hotels offer _____ services for their guests.
2. I _____ your company started in London.
3. I think the company is _____ Tokyo.
4. I wasn't _____ the area before I traveled there.
5. Katie _____ the receptionist, and now she's the CEO.

2. VIDEO WATCHING — CHECK YOUR UNDERSTANDING

FIRST VIEWING Watch the video of Rachel introducing her company to a new client, Donald. Answer T (true) or F (false) based on the conversation.

1. The company was started by two people. T ☐ F ☐
2. The company mainly manufactures plastic now. T ☐ F ☐
3. The headquarters of the company are based in New York. T ☐ F ☐
4. There are 2,000 employees working at the location in California. T ☐ F ☐

UNIT 11 *Meeting with Clients*

SECOND VIEWING
Watch the video again and fill in the blanks with the words below.

| a wide range of | over 150 people working | expecting you |
| were founded in 1954 | have 60 stores worldwide | |

Rachel introduces her company to a new client as she takes him to a meeting room.

Rachel: Welcome to Harvest Furniture Corporation. Are you Donald?

Donald: Yes, I am. I'm here for a meeting.

Rachel: I've been ①_____. Let me show you to the meeting room. Are you familiar with our company?

Donald: Not really.

Rachel: We ②_____ by Paul and John Harvest. The company started out as a manufacturer of plastic, but now we produce ③_____ furniture.

Donald: That's interesting.

Rachel: Also, we ④_____ and our headquarters are based in California.

Donald: Wow. I had no idea your company was so big!

Rachel: There are ⑤_____ at this location alone. Currently, we have more than 2,000 employees in our company.

Donald: That's really impressive. I'm excited to learn more about this company.

3. USEFUL EXPRESSIONS

Countable nouns and uncountable nouns

Countable Nouns (regular nouns)	Uncountable Nouns (no plural form)	Plural Only Nouns (no singular form)
location(s)	furniture	headquarters
manufacturer(s)	Scotch tape	clothes
office(s)	luggage	goods
employee(s)	paper (for the material paper)	congratulations

Scene 2 — INTRODUCING PRODUCTS AND SERVICES

1. LANGUAGE NOTES

WORD BANK Fill in the blanks with the most appropriate word from the box. Change the word form wherever necessary.

piece	handle	absolutely	estimate	factory

1. The _____ of furniture I bought last week still hasn't arrived.
2. I _____ agree with you on that.
3. Sam works in a _____ now, but he hopes to find an office job soon.
4. I couldn't _____ the stress of my job, so I quit.
5. Yesterday, Joel _____ that it would take two weeks to complete the order.

PHRASES Fill in the blanks with the most appropriate phrase from the box. Change the word form wherever necessary.

square feet	take a look	production capacity	amount of	depend on

1. I asked Linda to _____ at my e-mail before I sent it.
2. We need to complete this task in a short _____ time.
3. The factory's _____ was lowered after several employees left.
4. The prices will change _____ how much you order.
5. Do you know how many _____ this office is?

2. VIDEO WATCHING — CHECK YOUR UNDERSTANDING

FIRST VIEWING Watch the video of Donald having a meeting with a salesperson from Harvest Furniture Corporation, and choose the correct answers.

1. What kind of furniture does Donald want?
   A. Furniture that doesn't cost much
   B. Furniture that he can use in his office
   C. Furniture that was made a few years ago
   D. Furniture that will look good in his home

2. How fast can the company make new pieces?
   A. It takes three hours to make one piece.
   B. In one hour, they can make three small pieces.
   C. In three hours, they can make one very large piece.
   D. Three average-sized pieces can be made in an hour.

3. Why does Donald want to look at the catalog?
   A. To see how long it will take to make what he wants
   B. To estimate the amount he will have to pay for his order
   C. To look at the types of furniture that are available
   D. To find out how the company makes its furniture

UNIT 11 *Meeting with Clients*

SECOND VIEWING Watch the video again and fill in the blanks.

 2-02

Donald has a meeting with a salesperson from Harvest Furniture Corporation.

Connie: Welcome, Donald. I'm Connie.

Donald: Nice to meet you.

Connie: You're ① _____ for your office, right? We offer a wide variety of office furniture. I'm sure that we'll be able to find something to fit your needs.

Donald: I hope so. I need a lot of pieces made ② _____. Do you think your company will be able to handle that?

Connie: Absolutely. Our factory is over 60,000 square feet in size.

Donald: Great. How long do you think it will take to ③ _____?

Connie: We have a production capacity of three average-sized pieces per hour. So, it really depends on ④ _____.

Donald: Let's take a look at your catalog, and then we can estimate ⑤ _____.

3. USEFUL EXPRESSIONS

MAKING QUESTIONS Create questions for the answers given and practice with a partner.

1. **Q** Can _____?
   A Sure. We can easily handle large orders.

2. **Q** How long _____?
   A Our average production rate is 30 items an hour.

3. **Q** _____?
   A We have a wide variety of products available.

4. **Q** _____?
   A It's about 1,200 square feet.

5. **Q** _____?
   A Yes, I have a catalog right here for you.

91

Language Practice

Work with a partner and practice the sample conversation between a salesperson and a customer. Then create your own conversation, changing the underlined expressions.

Salesperson:	Welcome to <u>Lion Corporation</u>. Are you familiar with our company?
Customer:	<u>A little bit, but not really</u>. Can you tell me about it?
Salesperson:	Sure. We were founded <u>in 2003 by Sally White</u>. She started the business <u>at home</u>. <u>She came up with many recipes in her kitchen</u>.
Customer:	<u>That's interesting</u>. How many <u>branches does your company</u> have now?
Salesperson:	Currently, we have 20 branches in various countries and our headquarters are located <u>in Taipei</u>.
Customer:	How many employees do you have?
Salesperson:	<u>We have more than 1,000 employees worldwide</u>.

Company name:	*Fun Musik*
Established:	*2012*
No. of employees:	*30 (two schools)*
Products/Services:	*Entertainment/Shows*
	- music school for children (originally)
	- music and dance school for children and adults (now)
Location:	*New York City and Paris*

Company name:	*FashionforU*
Established:	*2020*
No. of employees:	*86 (10 stores)*
Products/Services:	*Fashion and Accessories*
	- street fashion for teenagers (originally)
	- casual and cool style fashion for everybody (now)
Location:	*Tokyo, Seoul, Beijing, and Singapore*

Language Function — Explaining conditions

~depend on NP or NP (S+V)

- *The service fees **depend on** the type of plans.*
- *The price **depends on** the number of chairs you order.*

Tell your clients that the price varies based on conditions mentioned and add a further comment.

1. (The price of the translation service / the number of words and the deadline)

   _____

2. (The price of office space / the location and the size)

   _____

3. (The price of shipping / the number of boxes and the distance)

   _____

Reading Comprehension

Read the following passage and choose the correct answer.

2-03

Whether they are large or small, whether they sell to the general public or to other companies, one thing almost all businesses have in common is the need to attract new clients. Effective marketing is essential to success, and businesses employ various methods in order to promote their products and services.

As technology has developed over time, more and more ways to reach new customers have become available, and the methods a company uses will depend on its target market and budget. For example, large companies selling products to the general public can go to the expense of producing television commercials. On the other hand, for many years, smaller companies were limited to methods such as advertising in local newspapers and delivering fliers in their local neighborhood.

However, the internet has changed all that. Even small firms can create their own company websites, and promoting products via social media such as Instagram can reach vast numbers of potential customers at a fraction of the cost of a TV advertisement. Marketing is constantly changing, and in order to be successful a company must make use of new techniques. Even so, one thing has remained the same: word-of-mouth marketing is not only very effective, but also free.

1. How many marketing techniques are mentioned?

    A. Four   B. Five   C. Six   D. Seven

2. What is the main reason that marketing methods have changed?

    A. The cost of producing television commercials has increased.
    B. Developments in technology have created new opportunities.
    C. Companies now need to reach a wider range of potential clients.
    D. Research has found more targeted marketing to be the most effective.

3. Which type of marketing costs the least?

    A. Social media marketing
    B. Television commercials
    C. Word-of-mouth marketing
    D. Advertising in local newspapers

Active Learning

Task 1

Choose one of your favorite TV commercials. Analyze it and tell your colleagues why you like it (e.g. slogan/tagline, concept, casting, visuals, music, setting/location, storylines/action, etc.) Then, based on this, brainstorm marketing campaign ideas for your client. You can choose the client's company/brand name.

Your favorite TV commercial
- Product Name
- Slogan / Tagline
- Concept
- Casting
- Setting / Location
- Music

Your idea for a new campaign
- Product Name
- Slogan / Tagline
- Concept
- Casting
- Setting / Location
- Music

Task 2

Based on your idea from Task 1, make a storyline for the TV commercial you'd like to make for your client.

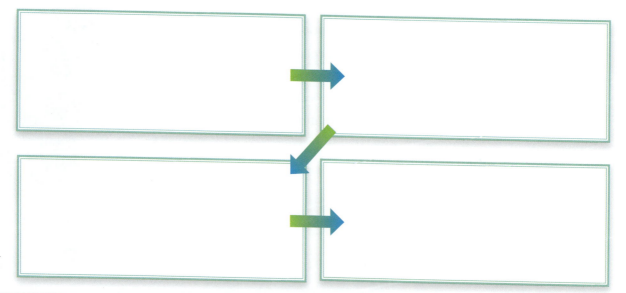

UNIT 12
Negotiations

✓ Checklist
In this unit, you will learn about...
- Asking for a better or lower price
- Confirming payment terms

Warm-up

Choose one of the situations below and use the cues given to role play a negotiation.

Outdoor Markets

How much are you asking for this?

Could you reduce the price to...?

Salary Negotiations

What is the salary range for this position?
I was hoping you could offer... (amount of money)

Business Deals

What's the standard price / your going rate for (product)?

What kind of discount can you offer?

95

Scene 1 — BARGAINING

1. LANGUAGE NOTES

WORD BANK — Match the following words with their meanings.

1. discuss
2. quote
3. lower
4. deal
5. steep

a. to offer a price for goods or services
b. contract, agreement
c. to talk over, to talk through, to debate
d. high price, costly, expensive
e. to decrease the price, to make it cheaper

PHRASES — Fill in the blanks with the most appropriate phrase from the box. Change the word form wherever necessary.

| willing to | place an order | a case of | at least | for now |

1. You will have to work for _____ eight hours on this project.
2. I'd like to _____ of 1,000 paper bags with you.
3. This is enough _____, but I might need more later.
4. Justin just bought _____ 500 pencils online.
5. Would you be _____ lower the price if I bought 2,000 of them?

2. VIDEO WATCHING — CHECK YOUR UNDERSTANDING

FIRST VIEWING — Watch the video of Owen meeting Terri and placing an order with her company, and choose the correct answers.

1. What does Owen want to do before placing his order?
   A. Confirm that his order is correct
   B. Discuss the prices that he was given
   C. Ask about other items that are on sale
   D. Check on the delivery times

2. What must Owen do to get a lower price on plastic bags?
   A. Buy larger bags
   B. Buy colored plastic bags
   C. Buy at least ten cases of them
   D. Buy two or more cases of them

3. What boxes does Owen decide to buy?
   A. The colored cake boxes
   B. The cheaper white cake boxes
   C. The more expensive boxes
   D. The discounted cake boxes

UNIT 12 Negotiations

SECOND VIEWING
Watch the video again and fill in the blanks with the words below.

  2-04

| the colored cake boxes | get an order form | you quoted me |
| lower the price | opening a bakery | |

Owen meets Terri at her company to place an order.

Owen: Hi. Are you Terri?

Terri: Yes, I am.

Owen: My name's Owen. I spoke to you on the phone.

Terri: Right. You're ①_____.

Owen: That's right. I'd like to place an order with you. First, though, I was hoping that we could discuss the prices.

Terri: Sure. What would you like to know?

Owen: Well, I think the price ②_____ for the plastic bags is a little high. Could you give me a lower price on a case of 1,000 bags?

Terri: Hmm. How about this? If you buy at least two cases, I will ③_____ of each by $10.

Owen: OK. Would you be willing to give me a better deal on ④_____, too? The price is too steep.

Terri: I'm sorry. The price I gave you before is the lowest I can offer.

Owen: Then I think I'll just get the white boxes for now, since they're cheaper.

Terri: OK. Let me ⑤_____.

3. USEFUL EXPRESSIONS

MATCHING
Match the responses with the questions/statements.

Question/Statement		Response
1. Would you be willing to lower the price?	▶ ◀	a. That's a great deal! I'll take it.
2. Could you give me a quote on paper bags?	▶ ◀	b. I want to know how much your cake boxes cost.
3. What would you like to know about our products?	▶ ◀	c. Sorry. That's the lowest price I can give you.
4. How about this? If you buy three cases, I'll give you a fourth one for free.	▶ ◀	d. Our items are more expensive because they are made from high-quality materials.
5. Why are your prices so steep?	▶ ◀	e. Sure. Colored ones are $2 and plain white ones are $1.

Scene 2 — COMPLETING THE ORDER

1. LANGUAGE NOTES

WORD BANK Fill in the blanks with the most appropriate word from the box. Change the word form wherever necessary.

finalize	confirm	apiece	tax	due

1. Your payment is _____ in three days.
2. Did you _____ your decision on the order?
3. The computers cost $1,200 _____.
4. I'd like to _____ my flight tomorrow.
5. The price I quoted included _____.

PHRASES Fill in the blanks with the most appropriate phrase from the box. Change the word form wherever necessary.

in addition	up front	by check	a balance of	by the end of

1. The product you ordered will be sent to you _____ this month.
2. Lisa was responsible for the project. _____, she had to lead the meetings about it.
3. After this payment, I will have _____ $200 in my bank.
4. You need to pay for your order _____, or we won't send you the items.
5. How would you like to pay, _____ or in cash?

2. VIDEO WATCHING — CHECK YOUR UNDERSTANDING

FIRST VIEWING Watch the video of Owen finalizing his order with Terri, and choose the correct answers.

1. How many cases of boxes does Owen want?
    A. 2   B. 3   C. 6   D. 9

2. How will Owen pay for his order?
    A. Pay for everything at one time with a credit card
    B. Make monthly payments with his credit card
    C. Pay for everything at one time with a check
    D. Make monthly payments with checks

3. When will Owen get his order?
    A. At the end of the month
    B. After he pays for everything
    C. By the end of the week
    D. This afternoon

UNIT 12 *Negotiations*

SECOND VIEWING   Watch the video again and fill in the blanks.

 2-05

Owen is finalizing his order with Terri.

Terri: Can I confirm your order with you?

Owen: Sure.

Terri: You want three cases of the 6-inch plastic bags, which cost $60 apiece with your discount. In addition, you want two cases of the plain white 9-inch cake boxes. They ①_____. Is that all correct?

Owen: Yup, that's everything.

Terri: Your total, including 7% tax, is $620.60. How would you like to pay?

Owen: ②_____.

Terri: Can you ③_____? Or would you like to make monthly payments?

Owen: Monthly payments would be great.

Terri: OK. How about ④_____ of $100, and then a balance of $20.60 due in the seventh month?

Owen: That's fine with me.

Terri: All right. ⑤_____. Everything will be delivered to you by the end of the week.

Owen: Thanks for your help.

3. USEFUL EXPRESSIONS

SHADOWING   Listen to the audio and practice saying the sentences below.

 2-06, 07

Talking about totals and discounts	
– That'll be $50 – Your total is $132	after tax (with tax / including tax). before tax (excluding tax / without tax).
– The cost of your order is $1,024 – Your total comes to $89	after the discount (with your 20% discount). before the discount (without any discounts).

Talking about payment terms	
– Would you like to pay	in one lump sum? in installments?
– You can pay	on delivery (on collection).
– Your charges will be divided	into three parts (into six monthly payments).

Language Practice

Work with a partner and practice the sample conversation between a seller and a customer. Then create your own conversation, changing the underlined expressions.

Seller:	I have your order ready.
Customer:	<u>All right. What is the total price?</u>
Seller:	It comes to $456 before tax.
Customer:	How much is it with tax?
Seller:	Altogether, it's $474.24 with the 4% tax. How would you like to pay?
Customer:	<u>By credit card.</u>
Seller:	Would you like to pay in one lump sum? Or would you like to make monthly payments?
Customer	<u>I'd like to pay everything up front.</u>

Different ways of payment

- pay **in one lump sum / for everything up front**
- pay **in installments** (e.g. in three monthly installments)
- pay **by credit card / debit card**   · pay **in cash**
- pay **by check**   · pay **with my smart phone / with a payment app**

Language Function   Negotiating / Asking about willingness

Would you be willing to V (infinitive)?

- *Would you be willing to* give me a better deal on the packages?
- *Would you be willing to* work overtime this Friday? We have a special event.

Ask about the speakers' willingness in the following situations and explain the reason you are asking.

1. (give a discount for the colored boxes)

_____

2. (extend the lease)

_____

3. (pay for everything up front)

_____

UNIT 12 *Negotiations*

Reading Comprehension

Read the following passage and choose **T** if the statement is true, or **F** if it is false. 2-08

Negotiations come in all shapes and sizes. World leaders negotiate with each other about political problems, parents negotiate with their children over bedtimes and meal choices, and of course in the business world, companies negotiate over prices, contract details, and many other issues. Whoever you are negotiating with, there are a few simple ways in which you can increase the chance of a successful outcome.

First, you need to decide on your goals. What is most important to you? And what points are you willing to compromise on? Thinking carefully about this before the negotiation begins is essential to achieving a good result. Next, it is important to be well-prepared. Research all the information you need and think about what arguments you will make to support your points. Predicting what arguments the other person will use and preparing your own counter-arguments in advance is also an excellent strategy.

Last but not least, remember that a negotiation is not a competition, but a cooperative process. The person you are negotiating with is not your opponent, but your partner, and negotiations only succeed when both people are happy with the result. If you only focus on what is good for your own company, then the negotiation will go nowhere. A win-win solution is by far the best outcome!

1. Good negotiation skills can be useful in politics and business, but not at home. T☐ F☐
2. To be a successful negotiator, it is important to know when to compromise. T☐ F☐
3. Setting goals in advance means it is hard to be flexible during negotiations. T☐ F☐
4. Before the negotiation begins, it is good to consider the issue from both sides. T☐ F☐
5. Competitive people who love to win make the best negotiators. T☐ F☐

Active Learning

Task 1

Your company is going to order 3,000 colored paper bags. One colored paper bag costs $2, so the total cost comes to $ 6,000. Email the manufacturer and request an initial 20% discount for a large order.

To:

Subject:

Task 2

You are at the negotiation table with your manager for an annual salary review. Note down your ideas below, then try to negotiate a raise in your salary. Explain to your manager how you have worked hard this year on some important jobs and what you'd like to accomplish in the next year. Work in pairs and switch roles.

Job responsibilities and achievements	Strong points and ambitions
-	-
-	-
-	-
-	-

UNIT 13
Giving Presentations

Checklist

In this unit, you will learn about...
- Giving a presentation to introduce your company
- Explaining tables, charts, and graphs

Warm-up

Match the situation (1-4) with the chart (A-D) that would be most suitable to display the information.

_____ 1. The changing values of two companies over a 10-year period

_____ 2. The share of one market, divided among companies

_____ 3. The exact money spent on specific items in one purchase

_____ 4. The total sales of different products for a company in one year

A Table

Product	Unit Price	Sales Volume	Subtotal
One-way switch	$3.00	125	$375.00
Two-way switch	$4.50	80	$360.00
Motor starter	$6.50	75	$487.50
Universal socket	$5.00	186	$930.00
USB charger	$3.50	68	$238.00
Total Sales			$2,390.50

B Line Graph

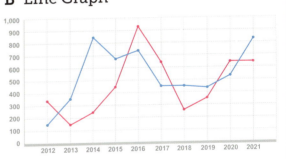

C Bar Chart

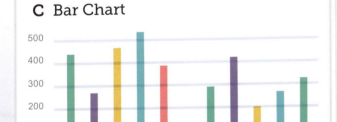

D Pie Chart

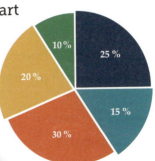

103

Scene 1 — GIVING A SUCCESSFUL PRESENTATION

1. LANGUAGE NOTES

WORD BANK — Match the following words with their meanings.

1. portrait
2. founder
3. notice
4. distribution
5. opportunity

a. to see, to observe, to realize
b. delivery, transporting
c. painting of a person
d. chance, occasion
e. someone who starts an organization

PHRASES — Fill in the blanks with the most appropriate phrase from the box. Change the word form wherever necessary.

start out as	break out	branch into	a household name	point out

1. It's important to remain calm when a fire _____.
2. McDonald's is _____ around the world.
3. The bank has now _____ selling insurance.
4. He _____ the problems his company had last year.
5. The fast-food chain _____ a single, small takeout restaurant.

2. VIDEO WATCHING — CHECK YOUR UNDERSTANDING

FIRST VIEWING — Watch the video of John, the R&D manager at Magnolia, introducing the company to visitors, and choose the correct answers.

1. What can they see in the lobby?
    A. A picture of the company's headquarters
    B. A picture of the company's foundation
    C. A picture of the company's original president
    D. A picture of the company's lemonade stand

2. How did Mr. Wallis get his start?
    A. Selling soda
    B. Selling lemonade
    C. Selling medicine
    D. Selling health products

3. According to the speaker, what helps the company succeed?
    A. Its R&D department
    B. Its location
    C. Its business plan
    D. Its employees

UNIT 13 *Giving Presentations*

SECOND VIEWING Watch the video again and fill in the blanks with the words below.

| natural health products | you may have noticed | branched into medicine |
| make this company successful | was founded in 1922 | |

John is the R&D Manager at Magnolia. He is introducing the company to visitors.

I'm glad to have the opportunity to talk to you today. First off, I'd like to explain a bit about our company. As ①_____, there is a portrait in the lobby. Well, that's our founder, Mr. Anthony Wallis, but everyone knew him as Tony. Magnolia ②_____ and started out as a one-man lemonade stand in St. Louis. Then Tony focused more on the distribution of lemonade and later on, lemon soda. When World War II broke out, Tony ③_____. By the 1970s, Magnolia was a household name. As you all know, Magnolia has now moved into ④_____. In wrapping up, I want to point out it is our 7,000 hardworking employees that ⑤_____.

We're finished for today. Thank you very much for coming.

3. USEFUL EXPRESSIONS

SHADOWING Listen to the audio and practice saying the sentences below.

Explaining about the company

1. This company was founded in 1954 by Joseph Williams.
2. We started out as a family hardware store.
3. Currently, we have more than 500 employees in our company.
4. We are headquartered in Boston.
5. We offer a wide variety of products and services.
6. Our specialty is flat-pack furniture.
7. We specialize in luxury carpets and sofas.

105

Scene 2	PIE CHARTS

1. LANGUAGE NOTES

WORD BANK Fill in the blanks with the most appropriate word from the box. Change the word form wherever necessary.

portion	represent	dominate	various	respectively

1. TechPhone has _____ the cell phone industry for years.
2. This line _____ the changes in the value of the stocks over time.
3. Emily and James are four and eight years old _____.
4. The biggest _____ of our revenue comes from retail sales.
5. We sell _____ items in the store we opened last month.

PHRASES Fill in the blanks with the most appropriate phrase from the box. Change the word form wherever necessary.

market share	web browser	account for	as you can see	second-leading

1. _____, the sales went down last winter due to bad weather.
2. Sylvia's sales _____ almost one third of the total last year.
3. Most people use one of the three major _____ .
4. Tom Hill is the _____ company in the tech industry as of this year.
5. The corporation's _____ is up five percent this quarter.

2. VIDEO WATCHING   CHECK YOUR UNDERSTANDING

FIRST VIEWING Watch the video of Janice explaining a pie chart. Answer **T** (true) or **F** (false) based on the talk.

WEB動画

1. The chart shows the market shares of web browsers from last year.   T ☐   F ☐
2. Web Pioneer has the biggest piece of the pie.   T ☐   F ☐
3. More than a quarter of users browse the internet with Flamecat.   T ☐   F ☐
4. Expedition and Awesome Online account for a 15 percent market share.   T ☐   F ☐
5. The green portion represents the browser with the lowest market share.   T ☐   F ☐

UNIT 13 *Giving Presentations*

SECOND VIEWING
Watch the video again and write the correct percentages in the blanks in the text and next to the pie chart.   2-11

This pie chart shows the current market shares of various web browsers. As you can see, the blue portion of the pie represents Web Pioneer, which dominates the market with a _____ share. Flamecat, in orange, is the second-leading browser at _____. Expedition (yellow) and Awesome Online (gray) hold _____ and _____ shares, respectively. All other browsers (green) account for _____ of the market.

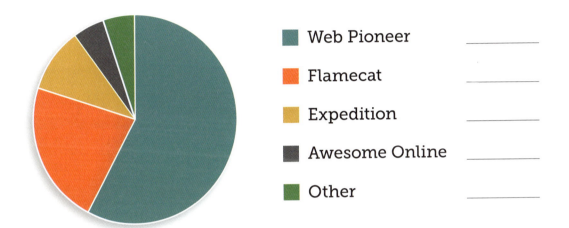

3. USEFUL EXPRESSIONS

SHADOWING
Listen to the audio and practice saying the sentences below. 2-12

Explaining about the chart

1. This chart shows the current market share of leading fast food restaurants.
2. As you can see, Happy Burgers dominates the market with a 60% share.
3. Happy Burgers has the largest piece of the pie.
4. Pizza2Go is the second-leading company at 18%.
5. Sam's Quick Chicken accounts for 10% of the market.
6. The orange portion represents all other fast food outlets.

Language Practice

Practice giving the following presentation. Then create your own presentation using the data given below and changing the underlined expressions.

On the screen you can see the sales report for the last two months. Firstly, the good news: following the rollout of our new <u>multi-colored post-it note pack</u>, sales <u>have increased by over 7,000</u> — that's <u>a rise of over 25%</u>. Also up slightly were <u>binder clip</u> sales, due to orders from a couple of big clients.

However, sales of <u>three-ring binders</u> took a dive, down <u>2,000</u> from <u>18,000</u> last year, to <u>16,000</u> this year. This poses the question of whether we'll actually continue to stock this product or <u>reduce the selling price</u>.

Product	The number of devices sold last year	The number of devices sold this year	Increase / Decrease		
Desktop computers	170M	122.4M	(-47.6M)	28 %	↓
Laptop computers	150M	177M	(+27M)	18 %	↑
iPads	130M	117M	(-13M)	10 %	↓
Smartphones	7.7B	8.6B	(+0.9B)	12 %	↑

Language Function — Explaining proportions

account for ～

- The use of social media **accounts for** more than 50% of fast fashion promotions.
- Electric vehicles **account for** 1.5% of the Japanese automobile market.

Explain the proportion of shares in the following markets and add a further comment.

1. (Sales of roses: 40% of the flower market in Europe)

   _____

2. (Sales of running shoes in Japan: Nike 18%, Adidas 9%)

   _____

3. (Shares of drinks: tea 24.3%, mineral water 17.8%, sparkling drinks 17.4%)

   _____

UNIT 13 *Giving Presentations*

Reading Comprehension

Read the following passage and choose the correct answer.

> For many business people, making presentations is something they do on a regular basis. Being a good presenter can be a great way to advance your career, so it is important to try and improve your skills. Firstly, think about your slide design. It is difficult to listen and read at the same time, so make sure slides do not include too much writing. Keywords, bullet points, and appropriate images are far better than long sentences. Also, if your slides include graphs, then keep them simple so your audience can easily understand the main point.
>
> Of course, good body language is also essential. The best presenters look relaxed and comfortable, rather than stiff and nervous. Most important of all, you should make eye contact with audience members as much as possible, and avoid looking down at your computer. Do your best to look at everyone in the room.
>
> Finally, remember that a presentation is not the same as a speech or a lecture, and a more interactive style often works well. Asking questions to the audience or sometimes making a joke can help create a relaxed atmosphere. Whoever you are presenting to, and whatever the goal of your presentation, these simple tips will help you do a good job.

1. Why is it important to have good presentation skills in business?
    A. Because you are more likely to get promoted
    B. Because presenting is something you will often have to do
    C. Because your audience are more likely to understand and enjoy the content of your presentation
    D. All these reasons

2. Which piece of advice about slide design is mentioned?
    A. You should choose your color scheme carefully.
    B. You should be sure to include all necessary details.
    C. You should avoid using graphs which include a lot of information.
    D. You should include an outline slide near the start of the presentation.

3. Which of the following is not mentioned in the passage?
    A. It is OK to use humor in a presentation.
    B. It is better if the presenter feels relaxed.
    C. It is important to smile and use hand gestures.
    D. It is helpful to include photographs on your slides.

Active Learning

Task 1

The total annual revenue of EX Company last year was 1 billion dollars. The pie chart below shows the percentage of revenue in each business sector. Explain about each sector based on the percentage you see in the pie chart.

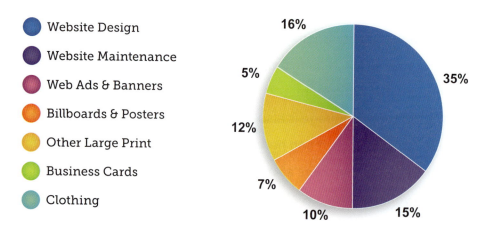

Note: Point out that the combination of web design, web maintenance, and web ads and banners was 60%, which shows digital work is dominating the industry now.

Task 2

Research a company you are interested in and find out about its profits in the last six months. Make a line graph like the sample one below, analyze the data, and give a presentation.

Note: Describe the profits either in dollars, euros, or yen.

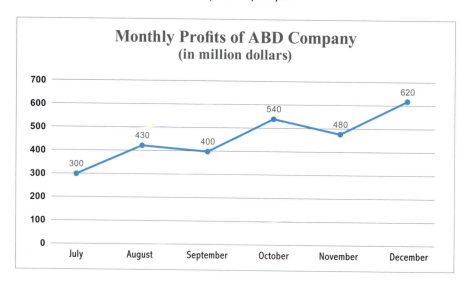

UNIT *14* Review *2*

A ▶ VOCABULARY I — Matching

Match the following words with their meanings. (There are two extra definitions.)

1. exaggerate •
2. pleasant •
3. client •
4. manufacturer •
5. quote •
6. founder •

• a. to offer a price for goods or services
• b. chance, occasion
• c. someone who starts an organization
• d. nice, comfortable
• e. to decrease the price, to make something cheaper
• f. customer, buyer, user
• g. to make something seem better than it really is
• h. a person or company that makes goods for sale

B ▶ VOCABULARY II — Gap Filling

Fill in the blanks with the most appropriate word from the box.
Change the word form wherever necessary. (There are two extra words.)

1. Can you tell us who the project _____ would be?
2. He reached into his bag and _____ the paperwork from the folder.
3. I get on well with all my new _____.
4. I couldn't _____ the stress of my job, so I quit.
5. Your payment is _____ in three days.
6. Emily and James are four and eight years old _____.

remove	impressive	handle	supervisor
due	respectively	luggage	coworker

C ▶ PHRASES — Gap Filling

Fill in the blanks with the most appropriate phrase from the box.
Change the word form wherever necessary. (There is one extra expression.)

1. People _____ be nervous before job interviews.
2. All the workers have two weeks' _____ a year.
3. I arrived a little earlier, but can I _____ now?
4. John is going to _____ our guests from Spain at the airport today.
5. Most hotels offer _____ services for their guests.
6. We need to complete this task in a short _____ time.
7. I'd like to _____ of 1000 paper bags with you.
8. It's important to remain calm when a fire _____.

head out	tend to	check in
pick up	paid vacation	place an order
break out	amount of	a wide range of

UNIT 14

111

D PHOTOGRAPHS

2-14~17

Listen and choose the sentence that best describes the photo.

1.

A.　　B.　　C.　　D.

2.

A.　　B.　　C.　　D.

3.

A.　　B.　　C.　　D.

4.

A.　　B.　　C.　　D.

E QUESTION AND RESPONSE

2-18~27

Listen and choose the best response to the sentence you hear.

1.	A	B	C	6.	A	B	C
2.	A	B	C	7.	A	B	C
3.	A	B	C	8.	A	B	C
4.	A	B	C	9.	A	B	C
5.	A	B	C	10.	A	B	C

112

F ▸ SHORT CONVERSATION

Listen to a short conversation and answer the questions.

1. Where are the speakers?
   - A. In the office
   - B. At the airport
   - C. At a market
   - D. In an airplane

2. Why does the woman want to take the man to the office?
   - A. Helen wants to talk about his account with him.
   - B. Helen wants to show him around the accounting department.
   - C. Helen wants to see him about her account.
   - D. Helen wants to try to bargain with him.

3. What does the man want to do?
   - A. Go to the office right away
   - B. Show the woman around the city
   - C. Relax while eating lunch with the woman
   - D. Spend some time in his hotel room

G ▸ SHORT TALK

Listen to a short talk and answer the questions.

1. When was Avian Air founded?
   - A. In 1945
   - B. In the 1960s
   - C. In the 1920s
   - D. In 1955

2. What did Avian manufacture before?
   - A. The company started out as a plane maker.
   - B. The company started out in headphone manufacturing.
   - C. The company used to produce cars.
   - D. The company made air conditioning units.

3. What will the company do in the future?
   - A. It will become a car producer.
   - B. It will open new locations around the world.
   - C. It will move its headquarters to another country.
   - D. It will fire some of its employees.

H ▶ INCOMPLETE SENTENCES

Choose the best word to complete each sentence.

1. I am writing _____ Black Tie Catering.

   A. on behalf of   **B.** instead of   **C.** on top of   **D.** based on

2. We are a catering company _____ in high-end corporate functions.

   A. specialize   **B.** specializes   **C.** specializing   **D.** specialization

3. Based _____ north London, our company offers a wide variety of cuisines, and we are available to work throughout the city.

   A. on   **B.** in   **C.** for   **D.** with

4. Our award-winning team of service people is well-trained, and there is no situation we _____ .

   A. can fulfill   **B.** can handle   **C.** cannot fulfill   **D.** cannot handle

5. We are so committed to _____ unbeatable quality that we guarantee a full refund to any clients who are less than satisfied with our service.

   A. delivering   **B.** deliver   **C.** delivery   **D.** delivered

6. Our food is _____ by top quality chefs who have experience working in Michelin Star restaurants worldwide.

   A. prepare   **B.** prepared   **C.** preparation   **D.** preparing

7. Please do not _____ to get in touch should you have any questions.

   A. feel free   **B.** look forward   **C.** feel happy   **D.** hesitate

8. The report _____ the different types of web browsers available.

   A. affects   **B.** compares   **C.** postpones   **D.** increases

9. This kind of product no longer _____ the market. It is old-fashioned.

   A. branches into   **B.** breaks out of   **C.** dominates   **D.** exports

10. Washington, Jefferson, and Jackson were the first, third, and seventh presidents, _____ .

   A. definitely   **B.** unfortunately   **C.** extremely   **D.** respectively

114

UNIT 14 *Review 2*

TEXT COMPLETION

Select the best answer to complete the text.

Dear Dawn,

Thank you so much for the free demonstration last Friday. It was nice to finally meet you
① _____, and the *DigiOffice* software looks like an excellent tool that I think our

  A. for good   **B.** on demand

  C. in person   **D.** from a distance

company would benefit from.

② _____, the price quoted is a little outside of our budget at the moment.

  A. Suddenly   **B.** Slowly

  C. Comfortably **D.** Unfortunately

However, we have come up with a possible ③ _____.

                                    A. solution   **B.** chance

                                    C. problem   **D.** budget

During the meeting, you mentioned that your company may be interested in
④ _____

  A. take advantage of   **B.** taking advantage of

  C. to take advantage of   **D.** having taken advantage of

some of our occupational therapy services. Therefore, we would like to offer you a deal of
30% off one of our occupational therapy packages for your ⑤ _____.

                                    A. employ   **B.** employers

                                    C. employment **D.** employees

Under these terms, we would send therapists to your offices twice annually, at the given rate.
In exchange, we would hope that you could lower the price of the software you are offering.

Best regards,

Samantha

UNIT 14

115

J ▶ READING

Read the following passage and answer the questions.

When accepting visitors from abroad, the golden rule is to put yourself in their shoes. From the moment you touch down in a foreign country, think about how you feel, and what you would like help with. One example may be that you're anxious about getting around the city, and first and foremost that means getting into the city from the airport. Others could be related to basic things such as taking care of internet, finding suitable things to eat, and communicating with the locals. In fact, that last one is a good reason to get an interpreter. This can also avoid misunderstandings with business issues, although interpreters are not cheap. If your company doesn't have the budget, choose the person in your office with the best ability to speak your guest's language. Finally, be sure to keep in mind the traditional customs of your guest's own home country, as they probably won't be familiar with all of yours. This also shows that you respect them and their culture.

1. According to the passage, what is the most important thing to remember when hosting guests?
   A. To help them set up an internet connection
   B. To imagine you are in your guest's position
   C. To help them get to know the local people
   D. To inform your employees of the guest's visit

2. Who can help you avoid misunderstandings, according to the passage?
   A. A local person   B. An interpreter
   C. Your boss   D. Your guest

3. What should you know about your guest?
   A. You should know what their budget is.
   B. You should know what their hobbies are.
   C. You should know what food they like.
   D. You should know about their culture.

MEMO

リンガポルタのご案内

リンガポルタ連動テキストをご購入の学生さんは、「リンガポルタ」を無料でご利用いただけます！

本テキストで学習していただく内容に準拠した問題を、オンライン学習システム「リンガポルタ」で学習していただくことができます。PCだけでなく、スマートフォンやタブレットでも学習できます。単語や文法、リスニング力などをよりしっかり身に付けていただくため、ぜひ積極的に活用してください。

リンガポルタの利用にはアカウントとアクセスコードの登録が必要です。登録方法については下記ページにアクセスしてください。

https://www.seibido.co.jp/linguaporta/register.html

本テキスト「English for the Global Workplace」のアクセスコードは下記です。

7312-2049-1231-0365-0003-0085-42CY-3C6J

・リンガポルタの学習機能
（画像はサンプルです。また、すべてのテキストに以下の4つの機能が用意されているわけではありません）

● 多肢選択

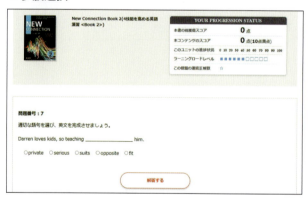

● 空所補充（音声を使っての聞き取り問題も可能）

● 単語並びかえ（マウスや手で単語を移動）

● マッチング（マウスや手で単語を移動）

Web動画のご案内　StreamLine

本テキストの映像は、オンラインでのストリーミング再生になります。下記URLよりご利用ください。なお**有効期限は、はじめてログインした時点から1年半**です。

https://st.seibido.co.jp

① 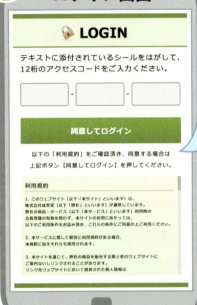 ログイン画面

巻末に添付されているシールをはがして、アクセスコードをご入力ください。

②  メニュー画面

「Video」または「Audio」を選択すると、それぞれストリーミング再生ができます。

③  再生画面

推奨動作環境

【PC OS】
Windows 7～ ／ Mac 10.8～

【Mobile OS】
iOS 7～ ／ Android 4.x～

【Desktop ブラウザ】
Internet Explorer 9～ / Firefox / Chrome / Safari / Microsoft Edge

TEXT PRODUCTION STAFF

edited by　編集
Minako Hagiwara　萩原 美奈子

cover design by　表紙デザイン
TRIDOT LLC　トライドット合同会社

text design by　本文デザイン
TRIDOT LLC　トライドット合同会社

CD PRODUCTION STAFF

narrated by　吹き込み者
Rachel Walzer (AmE)　レイチェル・ワルザー (アメリカ英語)
Howard Colefield (AmE)　ハワード・コルフィールド (アメリカ英語)

English for the Global Workplace
映像で学ぶ場面別ビジネス英語

2025年1月20日　初版発行
2025年2月15日　第2刷発行

著　　者　塩見 佳代子
　　　　　Matthew Coomber
　　　　　LiveABC editors

発 行 者　佐野 英一郎

発 行 所　株式会社 成美堂
　　　　　〒101-0052　東京都千代田区神田小川町3-22
　　　　　TEL 03-3291-2261　FAX 03-3293-5490
　　　　　https://www.seibido.co.jp

印刷・製本　(株)加藤文明社

ISBN 978-4-7919-7312-5　　　　　　　　　　Printed in Japan

・落丁・乱丁本はお取り替えします。
・本書の無断複写は、著作権上の例外を除き著作権侵害となります。